POCKET
EMPLOYER

OTHER TITLES FROM
THE ECONOMIST BOOKS

The Economist Desk Companion
The Economist Guide to Economic Indicators
The Economist Guide to the European Union
The Economist Numbers Guide
The Economist Style Guide
The International Dictionary of Finance
Going Digital

Pocket Accounting
Pocket Director
Pocket Finance
Pocket Information Technology
Pocket Investor
Pocket Law
Pocket Manager
Pocket Marketing
Pocket MBA
Pocket Negotiator
Pocket Strategy
Pocket Telecommunications

The Economist Pocket Africa
The Economist Pocket Asia
The Economist Pocket Britain in Figures
The Economist Pocket Europe in Figures
The Economist Pocket Latin America
The Economist Pocket Middle East
The Economist Pocket USA
The Economist Pocket World in Figures

POCKET
EMPLOYER

ELAINE ADKIN
GORDON JONES
PATRICIA LEIGHTON

THE ECONOMIST IN ASSOCIATION WITH
PROFILE BOOKS LTD

Profile Books Ltd, Registered Office:
62 Queen Anne Street, London W1M 9LA

First published by Profile Books Ltd
in association with
The Economist Newspaper Ltd 1997

Copyright © The Economist Newspaper Ltd, 1997

Text copyright © Elaine Adkin, Gordon Jones,
Patricia Leighton, 1997
Additional contributions from Pete Burgess

All rights reserved. Without limiting the rights under copyright reserved above, no part of this publication may be reproduced, stored in or introduced into a retrieval system, or transmitted, in any form or by any means (electronic, mechanical, photocopying, recording or otherwise), without the prior written permission of both the copyright owner and the publisher of this book.

The greatest care has been taken in compiling this book. However, no responsibility can be accepted by the publishers or compilers for the accuracy of the information presented.
Where opinion is expressed it is that of the author and does not necessarily coincide with the editorial views of
The Economist Newspaper.

Printed by
LEGO S.p.a. - Vicenza - Italy

A CIP catalogue record for this book is available
from the British Library

ISBN 1 86197 011 0

Contents

Introduction vi

Part 1 Essays
Hiring and firing … 3
Formalising the employment relationship … 9
The learning organisation … 15

Part 2 A–Z … 21

Part 3 Appendixes
1 Abbreviations and acronyms … 205
2 Useful addresses … 207
3 Other sources of information … 212
4 Publications … 214
5 Recommended reading … 216

INTRODUCTION

Pocket Employer is one of a series of books that bring the clarity for which *The Economist* is famous to the subject of management, in this case human resources management.

It is written by three experts in human resources, each with specialist knowledge, and is divided into three parts. Part 1 consists of essays which look at some of the crucial issues in employment practice and organisational structure.

Part 2 is an A–Z of the main terms that those who have a management position in an organisation should or may need to know, and which any employee will be interested in.

Sprinkled throughout this section are a number of quotations from both managers and pundits that help provide insight and a sense of proportion.

In the A–Z section words in small capitals usually indicate a separate entry, thus enabling readers to find other relevant information (although they should note that abbreviations such as IBM are also in small capitals).

Part 3 consists of a number of useful appendixes.

The Pocket Management series is designed to take the mystique out of business jargon in a stimulating and entertaining way. Other titles in the series include:

Pocket Accounting
Pocket Director
Pocket Finance
Pocket Information Technology
Pocket Investor
Pocket Law
Pocket Manager
Pocket Marketing
Pocket MBA
Pocket Negotiator
Pocket Strategy
Pocket Telecommunications

Part 1
ESSAYS

HIRING AND FIRING

Although it is a self-evident truth that an organisation can only be as good as the people who work for it, many organisations pay insufficient attention to how they recruit people. They sometimes hire people who are unsuitable and whom they end up wanting to fire. Some of the best practices in hiring and firing are discussed in this essay.

The hiring process

The recruitment process covers everything from identifying the need for a new employee to cementing the employment relationship on the first day of work. Having identified the need, it is vital to specify as clearly as possible what the job entails and what experience, skills and other attributes will be required of the job holder. A job analysis, resulting in the drafting of a job description setting out the principal accountabilities of the job, will fulfil the first requirement. This is then used to produce a person specification, which describes the ideal candidate for the job. If an organisation uses competencies, both documents can be competency based.

Finding people

The next task is to find suitable candidates. This may be done by advertising internally, for example, on noticeboards, or externally in local or national newspapers, specialist or trade journals, on radio and television, or possibly on the Internet. Alternatively, a third party could be used, such as a recruitment agency or search consultant (headhunter). Which route to follow might also depend on the country in which recruitment is taking place.

Candidates are required to tell you something about themselves before you decide whether to meet them. They can be asked to write a letter or send a fax with career and personal details in a curriculum vitae (CV) or résumé. Some employers ask each candidate to complete an application form so that the details of all candidates are presented in a common format. It is important that the questions on the application form comply with the equal opportunities legislation in the country concerned.

Selecting people

Suitable candidates can be identified on the basis of this written information, providing that equal opportunities (and anti-discrimination) legislation is observed. The next stage may be some form of assessment of the candidates. Selection assessment methods include one-to-one or group interviews, aptitude tests, psychometric assessment, handwriting analysis (graphology) and work simulations, or a combination of these in an assessment centre. Remember that selection is a two-way process; you also need to convince the candidate of the benefits of joining your organisation. Another important task is to ascertain what pay and benefits your preferred candidate will require to join your organisation.

It is good practice to ensure that several people are involved in the selection decision to minimise the effects of individual prejudices. More cynically, this also spreads the responsibility for selection mistakes.

Once the selection decision has been taken it is a good idea to identify at least one fall-back candidate, in case your preferred candidate declines your offer. It is often useful to approach your preferred candidate, perhaps by telephone, to say you are going to make an offer. This gives the candidate the opportunity to comment on any of the terms and conditions of employment before you get locked into written contracts. But be careful: a good candidate, recognising the strong position he or she is in, may use the opportunity to re-open negotiations.

Getting people involved

Once a candidate has formally accepted your offer, try to get the him or her involved in your organisation before the first day of work. This can be done by inviting the person to relevant meetings and sending copies of relevant correspondence as well as organisation literature such as newsletters. Before the person starts work, make sure an appropriate induction programme has been arranged.

Throughout the recruitment process care should be taken to respond politely and speedily to applicants. Good candidates will soon be snapped up by someone else. Those who were not chosen can still be good ambassadors for an organisation if they were treated with respect.

The interview

Interviewing suitable candidates is usually a crucial part of the recruitment process. It is a two-way process in which the employer is trying to find out something about the candidate, and the candidate is trying to find out something about the organisation. The employer's aim is to ascertain whether the candidate can do the job, wants to do it on the terms and conditions offered, and is likely to fit into the organisation.

The more effort you put into preparing for an interview the more useful it is likely to be. The person specification for the job is a good place to start. This indicates what skills, experience and other attributes are sought. The candidate's CV, résumé or application form will give a broad idea of how the candidate measures up to your requirements. The interview is the opportunity to fill in the gaps.

Interviewing techniques

Unless the job involves working under the pressure of being harangued and intimidated (as it may in some customer contact roles) and the interviewer wants to see how the candidate is likely to respond, it is usually best to conduct the interview in a relaxed and friendly manner. Your aim should be to encourage the candidate to tell his or her story. Similarly, your interviews should be conducted in surroundings that indicate how important the interview is. A messy office or telephone or personal interruptions are not conducive to an effective interview.

Open questions starting with what, why, who, when, where, how, tell me about ... usually elicit more useful information than closed questions requiring a one word answer, such as: "Do you like heavy rock music?" Leading questions, where the answer is implicit in the question, usually reveal little; for example: "You'd be happy to work the hours necessary to do the job, I assume?" It is best to keep questions short and easy to understand. Some interviewers ask such complex and convoluted questions that by the time the candidate answers (or not) they cannot remember what they were asked in the first place. Questions should not be unlawfully discriminatory, although individual countries' legislative requirements will determine what can and cannot be asked. In the European Union and the USA, for example, it would be unlawful to ask a woman whether she intended to have children.

Silence is often a useful interviewing tool. If the interviewer simply remains silent, perhaps smiles a little or raises one eyebrow, the candidate will usually feel compelled to break the silence. What the interviewee says then can be far more revealing than the answers he or she has been rehearsing. The aim should be for the candidate to speak far more than the interviewer, say, two-thirds of the time at least. Many interviewers enjoy the sound of their own voices so much that they find out little about the interviewee and may even put the candidate off joining the organisation.

One-to-one or a panel?
Interviews can be conducted one-to-one, in groups and/or by a panel of interviewers. One-to-one interviews can be less formal and more relaxed. A relaxed candidate is far more likely to divulge information about weaknesses as well as

strengths. A single interviewer has greater control over the process than several interviewers. However, with a panel of interviewers there is less likelihood of any one person's prejudices distorting the process. A panel can also combine people who have specific expertise in the various parts of the job in question and may thus be technically more competent to make a judgment than an interviewer working alone. This technical competence can be achieved by having a series of one-to-one interviews with different people, although each interviewer will have direct access to data from only one interview.

A panel interview should be carefully planned to ensure that the panel members understand their roles. The danger is that different interviewers may ask the same question (because one of them was not paying attention when another asked that question), or they may interrupt or even disagree with each other.

If the interview is being used to determine whether a candidate is worthy of more detailed consideration it should last no more than 30 minutes. If its purpose is to obtain more detailed information about the candidate then less than an hour is unlikely to suffice, and a longer period is often appropriate. It is not sensible for people to conduct too many interviews in one day. Interviewing demands constant attention, and fatigue will set in after a few hours.

Putting candidates at ease

It is important to spend some time initially putting the candidate at ease. More probing or challenging questions can wait until a rapport has been established. It is also considerate to wind down at the end of the interview so that it does not come to an abrupt stop, with the candidate out on the street wondering what has happened.

Opinions differ on whether notes should be made during an interview. There is a lot in the old adage that a short pencil is far more reliable than a long memory. If notes are made they should be brief, so that the candidate is not always looking at the top of the interviewer's head. Also, if the candidate is admitting to a weakness or talking about a particularly sensitive issue, it is better to wait until the interview has moved on to a less sensitive phase before making a note. A candidate may become nervous if his or her weaknesses are jotted down immediately, especially if nothing else has been noted.

The firing process

The other end of the employment cycle is when the employee leaves, which can be through resignation or dismissal. Dismissal is the most drastic form of disciplinary action and should be used only for the most serious offences. If an organisation decides it must fire someone because they are not up to the job rather than because they are guilty of serious misconduct, the employee should be allowed to leave with dignity, perhaps by being offered the chance to resign.

The dismissal process is complex and employment law requirements must be met. If an organisation has a human resources department it should be consulted to ensure that there is compliance with notice periods, legal and trade union requirements, and to avoid subsequent litigation for unfair dismissal. Consideration should also be given as to who within an organisation has the authority to dismiss staff. Because of the serious implications and consequences, most organisations, especially those that are unionised, allow only senior managers to carry out this task.

The employee may ask for a reference, which there is no obligation to provide. However, if the organisation wishes to help the employee find another job, providing a reference may help.

FORMALISING THE EMPLOYMENT RELATIONSHIP

The employment relationship takes many forms. It can be permanent or temporary, full-time or part-time, self-employed or employee status. It can be for a particular short-term purpose (task contracts); or involve workers based at home. In some workplaces trade unions are recognised by the employer for the purposes of negotiating the key terms of employment, especially pay, hours and benefits; in others unions have no role. In many countries in continental Europe recognition of elected workforce representatives, once chosen, is mandatory. There may be workplace trade unions with a bargaining mandate or works councils which have rights to information, consultation and participation in decisions affecting many areas of the business. In France and the Netherlands employers are required to take the initiative and establish works councils for their employees, although the requirement is only weakly enforced in the former.

Globalisation

An increasing number of people work for multinational organisations where the major decisions about employment are made outside the country in which they work. Organisational policies and culture have thus become more diverse in recognition of national differences, but at the same time have often begun to displace local practices in favour of a unitary corporate approach.

Employment relationships have become more complex and are increasingly affected by international policies and practices. Employment law, in regulating the framework for employment, has also become more international and more intrusive. The European Commission and most of the member states of the European Union have been concerned to develop a social agenda to accompany the opening up of the internal market, and this has contained a number of important binding measures affecting health and safety at work, working time, employee representation and data protection. In addition, the commitment to sex equality in the Treaty of Rome has had far-reaching consequences for employee rights in areas such as pensions.

Flexibility

Employers have many choices about who to employ and on what basis and terms. The latest fashion is for flexible employment relationships where the contract of employment reflects, ideally, the needs of both employer and employee. Hence the growth in fixed-term, part-time and outsourced employment, as well as job sharing, flexi-hours and some increase in homeworking. This flexibility and diversity has developed at a time when most countries have basic statutory protections, often involving pay, hours, job security and occupational benefits such as maternity rights. All legal systems, however, regard the basic employment relationship, formalised in the contract of employment, as underpinning those statutory protections.

The contract of employment

What is a contract of employment? The answer is simple; it is the legally binding relationship of work. An offer of work, however informal, creates a binding legal relationship, providing the parties clearly define what they want. For example, a simple conversation in a bar – "Do you want bar work?" "Yes." "£3.50 an hour?" "Yes." "Start 6pm tonight?" "Yes." – will create a contract of employment. A few matters will need clarification, such as hours of work, holidays, disciplinary rules, and so on, but the basics of an employment contract are there.

Having created the contract there are some consequences. The law recognises that a contract of employment is made up of two types of terms: express terms and implied terms. Express terms are the terms the parties articulate, such as £3.50 an hour for working in a bar. Implied terms are the terms developed by the law courts over the years to make the legal relationship viable. For example, it is implicit (implied) that if A agrees to work for B, B will expect the work to be done competently and A will expect to be paid at least the going rate for the work. A also expects the place of work to be safe, and B expects A to be honest. The law regards the relationship as interdependent and mutually beneficial.

There is a lot of case law on the nature of implied terms, but it is better to formalise the employment relationship rather than leave its interpretation to the courts. Most jobs today are complex and employers and employees like to know where they stand. For example, when they want to end the relationship they need to know if it can be done quickly or if several weeks' notice is required. Employees need to know how pay is earned and made up, what is expected of them, what rules apply to them and what disciplinary and grievance procedures are in place.

However, the most important reason for thinking through and clearly articulating the employment relationship is that since it is at the heart of the operations of a business, it needs to reflect and be consistent with the business's values and aims. Thus an organisation committed to flexibility, quality and customer care must implement these objectives. A healthcare organisation, for example, is likely to include rules on smoking at work in its contracts of employment.

Getting it right

Employment contracts and any accompanying documentation need care and attention. Using an off-the-peg contract or selecting well-worn phrases from a manual or precedent book may not satisfy discrete organisational objectives. Employees can detect a great deal from the language and tone of such documentation. A hostile and restrictive document from an organisation apparently committed to trust, quality and employee empowerment would arouse suspicion. Contract documents are not only used for legal purposes or to fulfil the statutory obligation to specify prescribed terms of work in writing (Section 1, Employment Rights Act 1996); they should also be part of an organisation's general communication system.

It may, however, be necessary to rely on the document to sort out a problem. It is easier to discipline an employee who looks scruffy or is rude to a customer if the documentation specifies the need for a smart and clean appearance and politeness to customers. Disputes about pay, overtime or commission can also be resolved more easily if the contract is clearly drafted. It is even more important to get the contract right where the employment relationship is more arms length or short term, such as when someone is employed on a freelance basis.

Contracts for the self-employed

An increasing number of people are self-employed. They may be called freelance or contract staff or some other label linked to a particular occupation. People who are genuinely self-employed are treated differently by employment laws throughout the world. However, these laws have often struggled to provide clear rules and guidance to help employers decide whether a particular individual should be treated as self-employed or not. A simple approach, favoured by many legal systems including that of the UK, is to ask whether the individuals in question are in business on their own account. If they are, they will not usually be dependent on one employer for their livelihood. They will hire out their skills, provide their own equipment, and so on, and take the risk of profit and loss.

Whether an individual works part-time, at home, or in a highly skilled occupation does not in principle affect the position. If in doubt, specialist legal advice should be sought. Advice from the tax authorities is generally helpful but not conclusive. The fact that an individual would rather be self-employed is similarly inconclusive.

If an individual is genuinely self-employed the contract still needs to be carefully drafted. Such contracts are likely to be short-lived, but this does not mean that the documents can be skeletal. The contract should:

- define the precise task to be performed;
- set the standards expected of the self employed person and the employing organisation;
- clarify the basis and timing of payment;
- detail procedures for delays and disputes over the work;
- deal with issues of equipment use, security, health and safety, confidentiality, intellectual property, and so on;
- include arrangements for premature termination.

The employing organisation should ensure that it remains in the driving seat regarding contracts with self-employed people. Poor consultants, freelance staff and others can damage an organisation's reputation. A well-managed relationship, by contrast, can enhance it.

What to put in a document

The law requires a minimum of written information for employees. Most of it should be in one document (a letter, memo or handbook as well as a document entitled Contract of Employment may suffice). It must include the names of the parties, starting date, hours of work, pay and when it is paid, place of work, job title, means whereby terms of work are determined (such as by collective agreement), holidays, arrangements (if any) for holiday pay and pensions, notice periods, disciplinary and grievance procedures. All employees who work more than eight hours a week must be given this information within two months of joining an organisation. If a contract is temporary, the employee must be told its likely length.

Most employers should do more than this. The rules for high-priority issues such as confidentiality, fidelity, hygiene, safety and dress should be clearly spelt out. Ideally, the document should explain both the reason for a topic's priority (handling money, access to secret or sensitive data, the job involves developing pharmaceuticals in a highly competitive market, and so on) and state what must not be done and the consequences if it is. As well as topics that are specific to an occupation and/or post, in most organisations there are others that need to be covered. These include the following.

- Terms relating to pay and overtime or enhanced pay, including performance pay. In all cases it is vital to state whether access to the enhanced pay is voluntary or mandatory (especially relevant to overtime), and whether bonuses, profit-related pay and so on are discretionary. If so, how are they earned and who makes the judgment?
- Terms relating to employer's rights, such as rights to search, require medical examinations, redeploy, use random medical checks and to require co-operation with health and safety measures.
- Terms relating to compliance with organisational policies, such as those on smoking, equal opportunities, dignity and quality assurance.
- Terms relating to occupational benefits, such as travel and other expenses, company cars, healthcare, financial assistance for training and gaining qualifications.

Such documents are a central part of an organisation's communication system. They should be well-designed, attractive and clearly written, avoiding jargon, legalese and undue complexity.

THE LEARNING ORGANISATION

In today's fast-moving world no organisation can afford to become complacent and operate on the principle of "that is the way we have always done it". There are always better ways to do things and they require new ideas, greater knowledge and a broadening of the skills base. The realisation of this gave rise to the concept of the learning organisation, which consciously and intentionally promotes learning as the primary route to a successful business. By focusing on learning, both individual and organisational, an organisation can find ways to provide better quality and better service at lower costs. An organisation that continually improves by creating and refining the capabilities needed for future success will, the theory goes, breed success.

The leaders of a learning organisation must set an example, creating a climate in which all staff are motivated to learn and thus develop their potential. As their personal performance improves, so does the performance of all aspects of the business.

Learning organisations are constantly changing. They learn from their mistakes; they value knowledge from outside and learn from their competitors; they benchmark themselves against the best. The competitive advantage gained by a learning organisation is the ability to learn faster than its competitors.

Success through learning

It is the label, not the learning organisation itself, that is new. Researchers throughout the world discovered that despite the rapid pace of change, downturns in certain industries and recession, some businesses were much more successful than their competitors. There seemed to be no reason for this phenomenon. These businesses, however, whether in the USA, Japan or Europe, had one thing in common. Their leaders had embraced change, and had consciously, or unconsciously, created organisations that are driven by learning.

Although most organisations have staff development programmes, research has shown that much development is merely a means to an organisation's end. This may not be intentional; it happens because the focus is on objectives such as achieving high market share or becoming the best service provider. The learning organisation subtly shifts the emphasis by seeing personal development as an end in itself. Organisations learn only through the individuals who learn, and although individual learning does not guarantee organisational learning, without it no organisational learning occurs.

The importance of feedback

There is another crucial difference between learning organisations and the rest. A learning organisation critically analyses everything it does, to identify what helps to create success and what mistakes have been made. Why? Because in addition to the creative element, organisations need to be able to adapt, often quickly. To do this they need to know what to do and how to do it.

Learning organisations constantly analyse everything: their policies, procedures, processes and projects. The audit is honest. There are no cover-ups to avoid loss of face or hurt feelings and no apportioning of blame. They need to identify the mistakes, the blind alleys and the not-so-successful approaches, so that the knowledge can be communicated and shared throughout the enterprise, and to ensure that such mistakes do not happen again. Wrong decisions are published rather than punished, so that everyone knows what has been tried, tested and failed.

Lesson one for learners

How do we persuade people to learn? This is not the issue in creating a learning organisation. Humans are learning and creative animals. They learn providing that there is emotion, interest, desire and a little pressure (but not too much).

How people learn is not important – babies learn to speak and young children are infinitely creative. Since learning is a modification of behaviour, it is more important to shape the direction of learning. People need to operate in an environment that encourages learning and communication. There must also be role models, starting with the top team.

Stretching roles

Learning must be enjoyable. To develop their creativity, people should be encouraged to experiment and be given recognition and rewards for achievement. Insecurity makes people fearful of failure or ridicule, inhibiting both themselves and any chance of creating a successful learning organisation.

People with challenging jobs need good interpersonal skills to become role models. They must be stretched, challenged and empowered. People without experience cannot march into a job and say to their team "Do this", because at this stage it is unlikely that they, individually, will have sufficient knowledge and skill to make sound, critical decisions. It is hoped that they will get the team together and say, "I'm new to this – please help me to understand", and then, "Now here's our next problem. How are we going to solve it"? This will provide learning opportunities as experience is gained on the job.

Embracing creative change

A learning organisation is constantly changing. First it is driven from the top to set creative change in motion; then it is driven from the bottom as empowered staff create change. Each change will have an impact on other parts of the business, which will then require change. Inevitably, some people will feel uncomfortable in such a dynamic situation. Equally, the broadly defined purpose of the organisation will appear vague to those used to precise and detailed plans. Thus detailed communication is crucial in order to promote understanding of what the organisation is and where is it going.

But how should such cultural change be managed? How should individual learning and commitment to the organisation be encouraged? Chris Argyris in his book *Organisational Learning* and Peter Senge in *The Fifth Discipline* both suggest that producing and learning must be inextricably entwined. As Reg Revans wrote in *Action Learning*, people learn more from doing things than from sitting in a classroom. Projects are one way of managing the change through learning.

Targeted learning: practice makes perfect

People learn from experience, but experience is a slow, expensive, random and unreliable teacher. What can be done to speed up and refine experience? Rather than ad hoc or occasional projects, researchers have found that many successful businesses have adopted a project culture in which they constantly create development and improvement projects. Creative ideas are examined and the best are implemented. Creative and skilled managers are then deployed to ensure that the ideas work. The projects are designed to advance the organisation's capabilities and follow a logical sequence. This means that the audit of one project can benefit the team working on the next.

Tools that promote learning

There are two basic management tools that encourage and guide self-development: empowerment and competencies. The concept of competencies is one of "knowing yourself". Competency profiles identify the areas in personal performance that need improvement and reinforce the desire to learn. Competencies also provide an organisation with common drivers and a common language for a more objective assessment of the performance achieved. This language will also aid the rapid understanding of the most important competencies required in a job, thus refining recruitment and selection.

Top responsibilities
For the last 90 years the role of the top management team has been the 3Ss: to design the strategy, structure and systems of the business. The first management structures followed the social hierarchy. Then came Frederick Taylor and his scientific management system, which fragmented and systematised everything into discrete functions, restricting people's natural creativity within tight procedures.

The growth of empowerment means that the people down the line will define the strategy, structure and systems, leaving the top team with the new role of the 3Ps: defining purpose, enabling process and developing people.

Part 2
A–Z

A

ABSENCE

People are absent from work for many reasons. They may have a statutory entitlement (maternity leave, JURY SERVICE) or a contractual entitlement (sick leave, HOLIDAY). The absence may be authorised (compassionate leave, training) or unauthorised. It is the latter that will concern managers.

Absence is commonly measured as:

$$\text{Lost time rate} = \frac{100 \times \text{total absence (hours/days) in the period}}{\text{Possible total hours/days available in the period}}$$

The higher the rate, the more absence will cost a business. A simple attendance record system, properly operated, will identify the incidence of unauthorised absence. Is it a general problem or does it relate only to certain individuals? If the latter, then the matter should be raised with them by their managers to determine and attempt to rectify the cause. For example, an employee may have a personal problem with which the manager or the company can help. Unfortunately, many managers lack the confidence or skills to confront such issues – a problem that clear company guidelines and training will help overcome. (See also LATENESS.)

ACAS

See ADVISORY, CONCILIATION AND ARBITRATION SERVICE.

ACCIDENTS AT WORK

Employers have a legal duty to take reasonable care regarding the safety of their employees. Accidents cost money and they may also lead to victims claiming COMPENSATION. In the UK, if a company employs ten or more people on its PREMISES, every accident involving an employee must be recorded. If it has five or more employees a company must publish a written statement of its HEALTH AND SAFETY policy and have staff on site who are trained in first aid. A company with more than 400 employees must have a first-aid room.

ACCOMMODATION
A job offering accommodation, common in the hotel, agriculture and leisure industries, is attractive to many employees. There are some jobs where living in is essential, such as those involving residential care, custodial and security work. Accommodation can be free or subsidised. But what happens if employees are not up to the job and their employer wants to dismiss them? Can they also be evicted from the accommodation? In the UK the basic rule is that if the CONTRACT OF EMPLOYMENT clearly specifies the need for the employee to live in and the accommodation is provided as part of the contract, loss of job equals loss of accommodation. It will be needed for the next job holder.

ACTION-CENTRED LEADERSHIP
Developed by John Adair while at the Industrial Society, action-centred leadership takes Henri Fayol's definitions of management functions and adds the teachings of Abraham Maslow (see HIERARCHY OF NEEDS) and Frederick Herzberg (see HYGIENE FACTORS). Adair states that leadership is about TEAM WORK; teams usually have leaders and leaders usually create teams. Leadership is defined as three overlapping circles: task (the need to accomplish a common task); TEAM (the need to maintain a cohesive team); and the individual (the sum of the need of the individuals in the team). Failure in one area affects the others. Adair is adamant that "leaders are made, not born".

> *Good leaders don't have to be charismatic; the three most charismatic leaders of this century were Hitler, Stalin and Mao.*
> Peter Drucker

ACTION LEARNING
The idea that people learn better while working than they ever would in a classroom. It was developed by Reg Revans and adopted by the Japanese in the 1950s and 1960s for their quality

circles. Revans is almost unknown in his own country, the UK, but action learning is well understood in Belgium and Germany.

ADHOCRACY

Originally used by the leadership guru, Warren Bennis, and subsequently adopted by Alvin Toffler, Henry Mintzberg and Robert Waterman to describe small project teams that operate freely across departmental boundaries.

ADVISORY, CONCILIATION AND ARBITRATION SERVICE

A statutory independent body in the UK whose aim is to promote the improvement of industrial relations. The Advisory, Conciliation and Arbitration Service (ACAS) can help both management and trade unions in various ways, such as providing advice and information on:

- preventing and resolving industrial disputes;
- conciliating in actual and potential complaints to industrial tribunals;
- promoting good practice (for example, it publishes various codes of practice and advisory booklets, such as *Discipline At Work*).

Most of its work is carried out by regional offices. ACAS charges a fee for conferences, seminars, self-help clinics for small businesses and some publications.

AFFIRMATIVE ACTION

A US term describing action intended to accelerate the process of achieving equal employment opportunity for all. A number of reports and programmes are used to eliminate DISCRIMINATION on the grounds of RACE and sex. In addition to those that seek to develop the operation of equal employment opportunities policy by employers, they include:

- equal training opportunities for managers and supervisors;

- training and educational initiatives for minority groups;
- the establishment of targets and timetables for the hiring and promotion of members of minority groups and women.

The aim is not only to increase the number of women and members of minority groups employed, but also to ensure that they are considered for all jobs in an organisation.

AGE

Many organisations include age guidelines among their other requirements when advertising jobs. They may seek someone under, say, 35 years old, in the belief that younger people are more dynamic and creative than older people; or they may seek someone older because they believe them to be more reliable and blessed with the virtue and judgment of longer experience.

There is no explicit LAW in the UK against discrimination on the ground of age, but age bars may be discriminatory against women. The situation is similar in the rest of the EU, although there have been legal cases in several countries where recruiting only young people has been held to be discriminatory. In the USA federal LAW prohibits discrimination against people aged between 40 and 70.

Age may be a relevant factor in deciding someone's suitability for a job; for example, there is usually a minimum age for people employed to serve drinks in a bar. But in other circumstances employers who specify age requirements automatically exclude themselves from the skills and abilities of those who fall outside the age limits they specify.

AGENCY STAFF

UK employers are probably the most frequent users of temporary agency workers (or temps, as they are usually called) in the world. Temps are not employees of those they spend their days working for and may or may not be employees of the agency. Effective use of agency workers requires:

- clear identification of the organisation's need for temps rather than in-house staff;
- realistic costing, not only of the agency fee but also the transactional management costs of liaison, induction, training, and so on;
- recognition and resolution of problems likely to be experienced by temps, such as fitting in, dealing with unfamiliar equipment or unfamiliar work practices, and even exclusion from the office party;
- careful monitoring of temps' performance, cost and impact;
- clear understanding of the legal rules.

In continental Europe most people placed on short-term task-related contracts by temporary work agencies are employees of the agency. It is responsible for paying them, deducting tax and social security contributions and, perhaps, negotiating minimum rates with trade unions. In many cases temporary employees become permanent employees of the agency and enjoy the benefits of permanent employment. In contrast to the UK, the use of agency employees is tightly regulated in a number of European countries, with limits on the length of assignment to a client company and other restrictions. In Greece and Italy agency employment is still forbidden.

Most HEALTH AND SAFETY rules apply to temps. These have particular relevance to DISPLAY SCREEN EQUIPMENT. There should be close liaison with the agency regarding health and safety rules and standards; for example, there is no point in an agency supplying a 60-a-day smoker to a client with a robust no-smoking policy (see SMOKING AT WORK).

Policies on employing temps should be regularly reviewed. If they have been used to avoid head-count rules or to circumvent strict budgetary rules they may provide a short-term solution but store up problems for the future. In some organisations the same temp may have been employed for several years at a high cost.

AIDS
This was the personnel scare of the mid-1980s. Although currently there is no cure and no vaccine, in all other respects AIDS should be treated like any other form of degenerative ILLNESS. Normal sickness procedures and rules should apply. It may be necessary to allay the fears of staff through information and training.

ALCOHOL
Attitudes to drinking alcohol at work or during working hours vary from organisation to organisation and country to country, but in general they have become more strict in recent decades. Some organisations ban all alcohol, even for entertaining guests, and may insist on stiff medical examinations of prospective employees to identify anyone with a possible alcohol problem. Others still tolerate the now much less common practice of long and liquid lunches. However, drunkenness at work may result in a DISCIPLINARY PROCEDURE, especially if it threatens safety or when someone is too drunk to do their job.

An organisation's policy towards the drinking of alcohol at work will depend on its CULTURE and the culture of the country in which it is operating. But whatever the policy is it should be clear to employees, and managers should take early action to deal with and try to help anyone whose conduct indicates they may have a drink problem.

Treat adults like naughty children and they will readily act out the role you have created for them!
Eric Berne

ALTERNATIVE WORK
See REDUNDANCY; MATERNITY RIGHTS.

A

ANNUAL HOURS

A contract where employees agree to be available to work for a fixed number of hours within a 12-month period and to work those hours when requested by the employer. Employees have the security of a regular weekly or monthly wage, regardless of the actual number of hours worked in a pay period, and the company is able to arrange their work schedules to suit its operational requirements. The arrangement is particularly suited to businesses that receive irregular orders, are seasonal, are in continuous production or operate in the services sector.

As well as a guaranteed and stable income, employees usually benefit from shorter working hours and a wider choice of the hours they work. For example, many continuous production companies that have adopted annual hours have introduced the five-shift system. Trade unions have welcomed the annual hours concept since it has led to improvements in working hours with no loss of security of earnings. The benefits for a company are greater flexibility, savings on overtime, better cover for absence, better retention and easier RECRUITMENT of staff, simplified pay procedures and generally increased productivity. It is, however, vital to work out the scheme carefully and provide for such things as illness, pregnancy, resignation and joining the organisation during the "pay reference period".

APPRAISAL

The process of assessing the development of an employee. Appraisal focuses on achievement and what needs to be done to improve it. It can fail when employers try to make it do too many things, but it should be used to help clarify what an organisation can do to meet the training and development needs of employees. The process is intended to facilitate communication between managers and employees, and it should provide a clear understanding for both of them of:

- the work that must be accomplished;

- the criteria by which achievement will be judged;
- OBJECTIVES;
- the process for giving the appraisee feedback on achievement.

Formal appraisal interviews should happen once or twice a year. This does not mean that managers should not talk informally to employees about performance, training and development issues during the rest of the year, which should be an ongoing process. The interview should be a summary of the discussions that have occurred during the year. Appraisal interviews can go wrong for a variety of reasons.

- The employee or the manager is unclear about the objectives of the interview.
- The employee and/or the manager are defensive.
- The manager exhibits bias.
- The employee or the manager does not adequately prepare for the interview.
- The manager talks all the time and does not ask open questions.
- The employee is reluctant to talk.
- The manager does not listen.

Some organisations use 360° appraisals by gathering, usually through a questionnaire, the views of peers as well as the appraisee's manager. This gives a view of the employee's performance from a range of perspectives and helps to eliminate personal bias. Care has to be taken in introducing such a scheme, as people may not be comfortable with receiving feedback from their peers and subordinates.

A badly conducted appraisal interview can be seen by the employee as being worse than not having an interview at all. For the appraiser there are some golden rules.

- Ensure there is a clear understanding by both parties of the purpose and

requirements of the appraisal interview.
- Ensure that feedback on the employee's performance is fair by pointing out the good areas of performance as well as those that need to be improved.
- Avoid generalisations and concentrate on specific examples of areas of good or unsatisfactory performance.
- Ask open-ended questions to elicit views and listen to the answers.
- Focus on how to resolve problems and improve performance.
- Agree actions that need to be taken and relevant timescales.
- Summarise the interview.
- Document the interview on the appropriate form.
- Follow up on agreed actions.

Ideally, the record of the interview should be written on a special performance appraisal form that is signed by the manager, the employee and often the senior manager. It is good practice to allow the employee to see the completed form and to add any comments.

For employees being appraised, the golden rule is to take advantage of the occasion to sort out any issues and to make their ambitions clear.

> *Communicate: telepathy has not yet been invented.*
> Anon

APPRENTICESHIP

Schemes under which school or college leavers and others are employed on a fixed-term contract that binds them to the employer and obliges the employer to train them. Furthermore, the employer cannot dismiss an apprentice for some of the reasons, such as a lack of skill, that it can other employees. There is no obligation to provide the apprentice with a job on completion of the contract. However, the employer should give notice of the expiry of the contract and be prepared to show that it had acted reasonably.

Apprenticeship schemes were the bedrock on which much of British industry developed its skills base, but they have almost died out in the past few decades. They are still prominent in some countries, notably Germany. To meet the decline in the old-style apprenticeships in the UK, the government recently launched the Modern Apprenticeships (MA) programme. An MA offers on-the-job training, leading to a National Vocational Qualification (NVQ). Typically, an apprentice will take between two-and-a-half and three years to complete an MA, which may involve anything from business administration to sea fishing.

APTITUDE TESTS

Tests used by an employer to help decide whether a candidate for a job is suitable. In theory, aptitude tests cover only natural abilities, such as manual dexterity, and exclude intelligence or academic ability. In practice, however, achievement and intelligence tests are often referred to as aptitude tests. An achievement test might be a typing speed test; an intelligence test would probably be a paper and pen exercise requiring the solving of problems that make use of words, numbers, symbols and abstract concepts.

ARBITRATION

A way of settling disputes that does not involve a law court or INDUSTRIAL TRIBUNAL. Most legal systems allow the parties to a dispute, especially where INDUSTRIAL ACTION is threatened or taking place, to seek a decision through an arbitration process. Arbitrators, often judges or very experienced people, are usually highly skilled, but they operate less formally than in a court of law. Their decisions are not legally enforceable, but if an employer who has voluntarily submitted to arbitration ignores the arbitrator's findings it is unlikely to do its reputation much good. In essence, arbitration can only work where the parties agree to the arbitrator's decision.

A

ASSESSMENT CENTRE

Companies that wish to review the development and potential of a group of staff, such as junior managers, often have interviews and assessments carried out at the same time by a group of trained evaluators in an assessment centre. The concept is also used when recruiting a number of staff at the same time, for example, management trainees. An assessment centre gives the candidates an opportunity to demonstrate their talents and the company a clear view of how they react under different conditions. It also allows a more detailed analysis than would be possible in a short interview. Individuals undertake a variety of exercises aimed at assessing a wide range of abilities and behaviour. These include written and oral communication skills, LEADERSHIP potential, person-management style, organisational and planning skills, creativity and initiative.

An assessment centre is usually set up at a company training centre or any other suitable venue.

Responsibility is the greatest developer of man.
Mary Parker Follett

ATTACHMENT OF EARNINGS

Under the Attachment of Earnings Act 1971, the High Court, County Courts and Magistrates' Courts in England and Wales can make attachment orders that oblige employers to make payments to the court from employees' earnings. Payments can relate to money an employee owes in respect of maintenance orders, administration orders, fines and legal aid contribution orders. Employers who make the payments can add 50p for administration expenses for each deduction. Employers who refuse to make a payment can be fined. Before or after issuing an attachment order a court can ask the employer to provide information about the employee's actual and anticipated earnings.

ATYPICAL WORKER

Jargon for any category of employee who does

not have an ordinary full-time contract of indefinite length (in other words, what is often called a permanent job). It includes part-time and casual workers, homeworkers, AGENCY STAFF and fixed-term workers, some of whom may be SELF-EMPLOYED. Such workers are also variously described as contingent, marginal, flexible or precarious workers, depending on how badly you consider they are treated. (See also FLEXIBILITY; FLEXIBLE WORKFORCE.)

BAD LANGUAGE

It should be made clear in a company's rules that specific sorts of behaviour (what we say and do) may be considered unacceptable and justify disciplinary action. Implicit in a CONTRACT OF EMPLOYMENT is an obligation that staff comply with the employer's reasonable instructions. What amounts to bad language is, of course, a matter of opinion, and a company would not want to draw up (let alone publish) a definitive list of words and phrases considered unacceptable. The best way to deal with the problem is to warn the employees concerned that their words or actions are unacceptable and should not be used in the workplace again. If they persist, a DISCIPLINARY PROCEDURE may be invoked. (See also UNACCEPTABLE BEHAVIOUR.)

BALANCED SCORECARD

A concept developed by Robert Kaplan and David Norton as a means of measuring and targeting organisational success. The authors claim that it is more than just a measurement system; it is a management system that can "channel energies, abilities and specific knowledge held by people throughout the organisation toward achieving long-term strategic goals". It looks at the business from four key perspectives:

1 Customer: how do the customers see us?
2 Internal: what must we excel at?
3 Innovation and learning: can we continue to improve and create value?
4 Financial: how do we look to the shareholders?

The process is forward-looking. It aims to get management to focus on the key issues facing the business and avoid the situation Theodore Levitt referred to when he commented: "Managers get wrapped up in the railroad, and lose sight that the customers are seeking transportation".

BANK HOLIDAY

See PUBLIC HOLIDAY.

BENCHMARKING

Defining standards of excellence for a product or process, against which future production or processes can be measured. For thousands of years craftsmen have studied the work of others with the aim of learning from and improving upon it. Benchmarking is a modern extension of this and lies at the heart of much management thinking about quality. Knowing that your products are uncompetitive is not enough; you also need to identify your weaknesses and strengths.

One way of doing this is to determine how other organisations are achieving their results and to identify what they have or do that you could successfully transfer to your operations. You must also determine what changes in policy, practices, CULTURE and behaviour will be necessary in the process. Your direct competitors are unlikely to give you much help, but similar processes often exist in quite different industries. For example, Xerox compared its warehousing and distribution function with that of a mail order company; Shorts of Belfast compared its autoclave function with a large bakery.

Once started, the process of benchmarking should, in theory, be continuous, extending beyond mere improvement. Your ultimate aim should be to become and remain the best.

> *Benchmarking is the continuous process of measuring your products, practices and services against your toughest competitors and industry leaders – then continuously improving to close the gap.*
> David Kearns, when CEO of Xerox Corporation

BENEFITS

The non-cash elements of an employee's reward package. Common benefits include, for example, paid HOLIDAY, pension contributions, DEATH and DISABILITY insurance, subsidised canteen meals or luncheon vouchers, private medical and dental insurance, free or cheap company products, a company car, subsidised loans. The list is almost endless. Benefits used to be an extremely popular and tax-efficient way to add to the reward package. However, the trend now is for tax authorities around the world to consider benefits as taxable income. (See also FLEXIBLE BENEFITS.)

BONUS

A way of rewarding individuals, teams or the entire workforce for their achievements. Bonuses are paid when specified OBJECTIVES, targets or standards are met or exceeded. They may be discretionary or contractual and are usually paid in a lump sum, monthly, quarterly, half yearly or annually. They may also be restricted to particular groups, such as executives or the salesforce. In Germany and the Netherlands there is a preference for individual rather than group bonus schemes, while in the UK and Scandinavia the reverse is true. Mediterranean countries rarely operate such schemes.

There are certain principles that should apply to a bonus scheme. It should be:

- based on clear, measurable, challenging and appropriate targets or objectives;
- designed to encourage employees to meet the needs of the business;
- acceptable to the employees;
- appropriate for the group(s) of employees it is covering;
- clearly communicated, so that all employees can understand how it operates;
- designed to produce payments that reflect the achievement of targets;
- paid on a regular basis.

BPR

See BUSINESS PROCESS RE-ENGINEERING.

BREACH OF CONTRACT

If you have agreed that someone will work for you, even for a few hours, a contract exists. It need not be written. The agreed terms can be broken and, in theory, if they are the "victim" is entitled to sue. LAW distinguishes between a simple breach, such as late arrival for work or a minor infringement by an employee of HEALTH AND SAFETY rules, and a so-called fundamental breach. The former entitles the victim to claim for compensation; the latter can rapidly end the relationship. If, for example, an employer fails to pay wages, demotes or disciplines an employee with no reason, or the employee takes away company secrets or company equipment, the relationship has broken down. The law accepts that the contract cannot go on if the innocent party does not wish it to. The employer is entitled to summarily (instantly) dismiss an employee in fundamental breach of contract without giving NOTICE; similarly, if the employer is in breach the employee can walk out and will probably win a claim for UNFAIR DISMISSAL, based on CONSTRUCTIVE DISMISSAL.

There can be a fine dividing line between a simple breach and a fundamental breach. Something an employer finds unacceptable, such as wearing earrings, RUDENESS or being insubordinate, may be viewed differently by a court of law. There is a risk, therefore, in a quick response; an employee might win an action for unfair dismissal. Similarly, an employee must be cautious when walking out since this also may not be legally justified. The moral is that everyone should avoid a knee-jerk reaction to a particular problem.

Breach of contract claims regarding employment cases can be taken to the ordinary courts and, increasingly in the UK, industrial tribunals. An INDUSTRIAL TRIBUNAL can only deal with cases which legislation empowers it to hear, such as unfair dismissal. However, where such a claim is made the tribunal can also deal with breach of contract claims. Employees often have a choice of where to bring a case, but they cannot pursue option two if they have already lost their case in option one.

BULLYING

The Manufacturing Science and Finance (MSF) union in the UK defines bullying as "persistent, offensive, abusive, intimidating, malicious or insulting behaviour, abuse of power or unfair penal sanctions, which makes the recipient feel upset, threatened, humiliated or vulnerable, which undermines their self-confidence and which may cause them to suffer STRESS". It is a widespread and worldwide problem at work. According to a 1994 study by Staffordshire University in the UK, 78% of a sample of 1,137 UK employees had witnessed bullying at their workplace and 51% had experienced it themselves.

The UK has no specific legislation to deal with bullying. However, UK employers have a duty to protect employees' health, safety and welfare at work, a common-law duty of care under the LAW of negligence and a statutory duty under the Health and Safety at Work Act. Many court actions concerning bullying have found companies "in breach of mutual trust and confidence". Where employees have resigned rather than continuing to suffer bullying, many claims for CONSTRUCTIVE DISMISSAL have been upheld.

Much of the bullying is of subordinates by their immediate superior, which can make it difficult for a company to identify that bullying is happening. It also makes it essential that the organisation's grievance procedures enable a bullied employee to complain to a person other than their immediate superior without fear of DISCRIMINATION, VICTIMISATION or further bullying.

The European Commission is concerned that bullying and similar problems will not be solved without some sort of legislation, and it has made a Recommendation on DIGNITY AT WORK. (See also HARASSMENT; UNACCEPTABLE BEHAVIOUR.)

BUSINESS CHANGE

New products, new PREMISES and new opening or business hours are required at some time by most employers. Sometimes the change is more radical, for example with takeovers and mergers. Change is frightening for most people and often resisted. Whatever the nature and scale of change it must be carefully planned for, and employees consulted and involved. The reasons for change, such as increased efficiency or flexibility, ought to be carefully explained. Poorly managed business changes are the most common cause of INDUSTRIAL ACTION.

There are legal rules covering business changes. Any change to employees' terms of work must be carried out lawfully (see CHANGING TERMS OF WORK). Usually, this will mean consultation and agreement with individual employees (or, if appropriate, their union). The theory advocating "give them NOTICE and then offer them new contracts" may be attractive, but it carries the risk that someone will challenge the changes, as does "we'll force it through and hope for the best". In both cases employees may be able to claim for UNFAIR DISMISSAL and/or BREACH OF CONTRACT. Employees are becoming more litigious and the trouble and costs of defending claims is high.

In much of continental Europe legally anchored rights for workplace employee REPRESENTATIVES require employers to provide extensive information on any proposed changes as well as allowing enforceable participation rights on many aspects of the implementation of change. In Germany, for example, all transfers of employees must be agreed with the WORKS COUNCIL, as must any changes in the organisation of working hours.

Traditionally, industrial tribunals in the UK have been sympathetic to employers who can show a genuine organisational reason for change aimed at improved competitiveness, productivity, flexibility, and so on. Cases tend to be lost because of mistakes by the employer, such as failure to consult, to explore options and to reduce problems for individual employees. The LAW rarely gets involved in why changes happen, but it does look closely at how they are handled.

Where change is to the nature of the employer itself, such as the merger of two firms, contracting out particular functions or going into receivership, the law imposes some detailed and demanding rules. In the European Union the law explicitly protects the employees affected. Basically, they move with the business, and any transfer should not offer grounds to worsen the terms and conditions of employment. In the UK, under the Transfer of Undertakings (Protection of Employment) Regulations 1981 (TUPE), a new owner (however arrived at) is required to maintain the terms of employees' contracts of employment. This may mean that an employer has two categories of staff – its original workforce and the TUPE employees – who are likely have different PAY, BENEFITS and conditions. Harmonising the employment terms of these groups must be undertaken gradually and lawfully, or it could lead to REDUNDANCY and claims of UNFAIR DISMISSAL. Current advice is that TUPE employees can hold on to their original contract terms for at least one year. All the legal liabilities have to be borne by the new owner. It is vital that companies considering OUTSOURCING, mergers or takeovers should take into account the costs of employee consultation and other issues associated with TUPE.

> *If we don't change direction, we are likely to end up where we are headed.*
> Chinese proverb

BUSINESS LINK

Set up in the UK as local one-stop shops to provide practical advice and help for businesses, Business Link centres are funded by the TRAINING AND ENTERPRISE COUNCILS. They provide paid-for consultancy, diagnostic and problem-solving services through the Register of Accredited Service Providers, as well as free economic, industry and marketing information, credit ratings, company information and even mailing lists. The Department of Trade and Industry has put £35m of extra funding into the Information Society Initiative to promote the benefits of using information and communications technologies in the UK.

BUSINESS PROCESS RE-ENGINEERING

A label given to the redesign of an organisation, first articulated by Michael Hammer and James Champy in their 1993 book *Re-engineering the Corporation*. Business process re-engineering (BPR) was described as the "radical redesign of business processes to achieve dramatic improvements in performance". The following three words were emphasised.

1 Radical: go back to the root of the process rather than merely improve what exists.
2 Processes: re-engineering is not just an organisational review, or even a review of the business, it is a review of the processes. It invariably means redesigning the organisation from a function-oriented structure to a process-organised structure.
3 Dramatic: the search is for quantum leaps, not just incremental improvement.

BPR is not about change for change's sake; it is about a willingness to accept risk and change when necessary. It is not about re-engineering a function; it is about re-engineering the work that the people in the function do. It is about rethinking the whole business. To use a well-known US expression, it is about "starting over". It became popular because many chief executives knew that successful business was about getting the process flow right, and that historical functions with their rigid boundaries were frustrating creativity and rapid change. There have been many success stories as well as many disappointments. Research in the USA and in the UK has identified some common indicators of success and failure.

The common failure factors were:

- inadequate LEADERSHIP from the top;
- unrealistic expectations;
- middle management resistance;
- the wrong person leading the project;
- the task delegated totally to technical consultants;

- failure to consider the human resources implications;
- paralysis by analysis; and
- fear of failure.

The preconditions for success were:

- total commitment from the top;
- realistic expectations;
- a realistic timescale;
- shared VISION;
- staff involvement; and
- cultural change to match the process change.

Many people are sceptical about BPR. Hammer's advice to "start over" ignores the good things currently being achieved. Few companies are willing revolutionaries; they may tinker with the structure but they will not demolish it.

BPR has cost many jobs in recent years, and much of the lack of success is because the implementers have ignored the human factor. Champy and Hammer do not disagree, and Champy now wants to re-engineer management.

We are all prisoners of our past. It's hard to think of things except in the way we have always thought of them. But that solves no problems and seldom changes anything.
Charles Handy

CAPABILITY

The ability of an employee to achieve the required standards of job performance. Where someone is failing to do this, many companies simply invoke a DISCIPLINARY PROCEDURE, but others deal with the matter through a capability policy founded on the principle that the carrot is better than the stick at influencing behaviour.

The policy should require the

- company to review its selection criteria and interview skills, and its training and support programmes;
- line manager to establish a programme of training and COACHING for the employee, with agreed achievement targets over time.

If the policy fails to help develop another capable employee, it will, at least, help establish the facts that will justify DISMISSAL on grounds of incapability as covered by the Employment Rights Act 1996.

CAREER ANCHORS

A term coined by Edgar Schein of the Massachusetts Institute of Technology (MIT) to denote the perceptions that individuals have about themselves in their jobs and which encourage them to stay in those jobs. The anchors were defined as: technical, managerial, creative, security and autonomy. Schein noted that in their early careers individuals adapt their behaviour to that of their organisation to such a degree that they become anchored to it (see PSYCHOLOGICAL CONTRACT.)

CAREERS SERVICES

There have always been private companies to help people identify and channel their expertise and latent talent towards a suitable career. There was also the Labour Exchange (now called the JOBCENTRE), which offered career counselling and advice, usually starting while people were in secondary education.

The careers services component of UK jobcentres has been privatised. Many of the new careers services companies are spin-offs from the TRAINING AND ENTERPRISE COUNCILS (TECs) and still work closely with the 81 UK TECs and 22 Scottish Local Enterprise Companies (LECs). They have an initial five-year contract with the government to provide core careers services, plus the opportunity to develop commercial services relevant to the needs of their local area. The companies have a duty to keep in touch with the local labour market and the needs of local employers, to support partnerships between local employers and educational establishments, to inform employers of the services available, to ensure a correct understanding of the current educational and vocational QUALIFICATIONS available, and to maintain details of training providers. They also operate placement and referral services, pre-selecting candidates against an employers' job specifications.

The Youth Training Scheme (YTS) concept continues, although usually under a new name. Two new initiatives – Modern Apprenticeships and National Traineeship – have been introduced and are marketed and administered by the new careers services companies. UK schools have a duty to arrange work experience for every pupil in year 11 (age 15–16). Some make direct arrangements with employers and others use the careers services companies.

Commercial services offered by such companies include outplacement counselling, individual PERSONAL DEVELOPMENT and further education programmes, many of which are subsidised.

CASUAL WORKER

A person employed intermittently and/or on a short-term basis. Casual workers may be employees or SELF-EMPLOYED (see EMPLOYMENT STATUS); it should not be assumed they are self-employed. There are many complex legal rules applying to such workers relating to, for example, statutory SICK PAY (SSP) and employment rights (see FIXED-TERM CONTRACT). Although casuals are apparently cheap to employ it is important to weigh up the real costs in time and money of the training and supervision they require, their productivity and the administrative burden. Using one casual employee for one day can cause havoc in a business, but casuals can be used effectively if the following are considered.

- Do they have the skills needed?
- Are they competent and reliable?
- Are managers trained and experienced in dealing with these "as and when" staff?
- Is appropriate information about the business, its rules and expectations readily available to casual workers?

CHANGING TERMS OF WORK

A term of a contract can only be changed in a lawful manner, even if the need for the change appears obvious; for example, longer shop opening hours, which is likely to affect current employees, or the introduction of new technology, which will affect the way people work, the skills they need and how they use them. Two things sensible employers can do to avoid INDUSTRIAL ACTION or the risk of a claim for BREACH OF CONTRACT or CONSTRUCTIVE DISMISSAL are as follows.

1 Check the written CONTRACT OF EMPLOYMENT (not the STATEMENT OF TERMS OF WORK) to ensure that what is being proposed is contractually allowed. If the written contract says, for example, that hours may be varied after giving no less than seven days' NOTICE, the employer can go ahead. If the contract specifies the mechanism of change it must be followed.

2 If the contract does not authorise change, there must be agreement to it, preferably in writing. Employees who carry on working cannot be assumed to have agreed; they still have the right to refuse.

Employers should not assume that because they have reached agreement with a TRADE UNION their employees, whether union members or not, will agree to the change.

CHECK OFF
An agreement between an employer and a recognised TRADE UNION to deduct union subscriptions from its employees' REMUNERATION and pay them to the union. The employees concerned must give written authorisation, which lasts for three years unless revoked, to their employer to make the deduction.

CLIMATE SURVEY
See EMPLOYEE OPINION SURVEY.

CLOSED SHOP
Where an applicant for a job or an employee must be, or must become, a member of a trade union recognised by the employer. In the UK closed shops used to be widespread and dominated such industries as printing. They are now illegal in the UK and forbidden in most European countries on the constitutional ground of freedom of association.

COACHING
Unlocking people's potential to help them maximise their own performance; helping them learn, rather than teaching them. Coaching staff has always been an important part of a manager's role, although regrettably one that may be pushed aside when production problems threaten the bottom line. With the advent of junior staff EMPOWERMENT, a large element of monitoring and controlling has been removed from management. The principle now should perhaps be to ask staff: "How can I help you achieve your objectives?"

> *In a hierarchy every employee tends to rise to his own level of incompetence.*
> Laurence J. Peter, *The Peter Principle*, 1969

COLLECTIVE BARGAINING
The process of setting pay and conditions of employment through negotiation between an employer or group of employers and employee REPRESENTATIVES acting on behalf of a group of

employees. Collective bargaining culminates in a collective agreement setting out the results of the negotiations and the rights and obligations of the parties involved. In the UK collective agreements are not legally binding unless they become incorporated into the individual's contract of employment. In most other jurisdictions a collective agreement not only imposes obligations on the employer and employee but also establishes a legal bond between the TRADE UNION negotiating the agreement and the signatory employer or employers' association. As a result, trade unions are often required to maintain industrial peace during the lifetime of an agreement.

The existence of both elected works councils and trade unions in countries such as France, Germany, the Netherlands and Spain necessitates an explicit division of bargaining authority between the two bodies. In most cases trade unions have an exclusive right to negotiate on terms and conditions (at national, regional or workplace level), with elected works councils, which represent both union and non-union employees, having consultation rights.

Under the UK Trade Union and Labour Relations (Consolidation) Act 1992, collective bargaining takes place over the following:

- Terms and conditions of employment, including physical working conditions
- Engagement, non-engagement, termination or the suspension of employment or duties
- Allocation of work or duties
- Staff discipline
- Membership or non-membership of a trade union
- Facilities for trade union officials
- The process for negotiation or consultation and other procedures relating to the above

Unions have no negotiation rights on matters not covered by the above. An employer may also refuse to negotiate on any issues for which it does not recognise the union for collective bargaining purposes.

Sometimes collective bargaining takes place at industry level. National joint councils are formed comprising employers' and trade unions' representatives. The agreements reached apply to all employers and employees on whose behalf the negotiations have been conducted. Statements of written particulars of employment, which cover the main terms and conditions of employment for all employees, irrespective of trade union membership, refer to collective agreements, but employees who are not union members can refuse to accept the terms collectively agreed.

Multi-employer bargaining, either nationally or regionally by industry, remains the norm throughout most of continental Europe, covering 70–90% of the workforce, although in France national and regional agreements are often seen as a minimum with employers negotiating or unilaterally determining improvements at workplace level. In contrast, negotiating on a company-by-company basis is now common in the UK, following the break-up of many industry agreements in the 1980s and the privatisation and fragmentation of former public utilities. However, multi-employer bargaining is under threat in most countries, with pressures to allow agreements to be made more flexible to accommodate local company needs and difficulties.

Authority in an organisation only exists in so far as the people in that organisation are willing to accept it.
Chester Barnard, president, Bell Telephone

COMMISSION PAYMENT

A performance-related payment. Many sales staff are paid a commission that is dependent on their performance. Some companies pay a low basic SALARY and a high commission; some pay an average to good salary and a low commission; and some pay only commission. According to research carried out in the UK by the Institute of Personnel Development (IPD), commission payments have the following advantages for employers.

- Pay is linked purely to sales volumes or profitability.
- Sales representatives may be SELF-EMPLOYED.
- Payments generally keep up with inflation and are therefore attractive to sales representatives.
- Only successful sales representatives stay with the company.
- Remuneration of sales staff is related to profits.
- Different commission rates can be paid for different products.
- Payments can be designed to be easy to administer and monitor.

They also have the following disadvantages.

- Lack of security in respect of pay may cause stress to sales staff and make it more difficult to recruit and retain them.
- Badly designed schemes may result in managers having little control over earnings.
- Sales representatives may be tempted to overload customers with stock, promoting items they may not need.
- Non-selling activities take second place.

COMMON LAW
See LAW.

COMMUNICATION CHANNELS
The means whereby organisations and their employees communicate with each other. Effective communication and CONSULTATION within an organisation are crucial to its success. Employees, wherever they are in the hierarchy, perform best if they know what is expected of them, what their powers are and what opportunities there are to make their views known on issues that concern them. Good communication also helps employees feel involved in and valued by a company.

Managers should remember that it is estimated

that people remember only 20% of what they hear, but probably more than 50% of what they see and hear. Worse, they make assumptions if there is no communication. This is a good enough reason to have a basic STAFF HANDBOOK to supplement the formal CONTRACT OF EMPLOYMENT, together with other written, or visual, forms of communication, such as journals and newsletters, department bulletins, notice boards, e-mail and individual letters to all employees. Personal contact, for example through group or inter-departmental meetings, is equally important, not least because it allows immediate response and interaction.

The meaning of communication is its effect.
Anon

COMPANY CARS

These account for more than 50% of all car sales in the UK and an increasing number throughout the rest of Europe. After a pension, a company car is now the most valuable employment benefit in Europe. The percentage of "status" cars compared with "genuine need" cars has never been accurately measured, but observers suggest that status cars account for over 30% of the total.

For employers, there are some important aspects of company car fleet ownership to consider.

1 Objective analysis will help develop the provisioning policy. For example, what:

- is the role of the car?
- are the business OBJECTIVES?
- are the market trends in car provision and policy?
- is the best financing strategy?
- is the ability to control costs?
- is the scope for flexibility and how should it be provided?
- are the relevant employee considerations?

2 The provision options are:

- buy the cars and do the administration yourself;
- buy the cars and outsource the administration;
- lease the cars and do some of the administration yourself;
- outsource everything.

3 Whichever option is chosen, the assessment should be made using "whole-life" costs; that is, the costs of running and maintaining the vehicle during its whole life with the company, including depreciation and resale value.

4 Check out the offers. With around 70% of their production going to fleet sales, the big European car manufacturers offer valuable extras, such as free careful driver training coupled with special insurance deals.

5 Make sure sufficient management resources are allocated to the task of running the fleet. Even if the job has been outsourced, someone needs to see how well it is being done. Fleet managers should get the appropriate fleet asset management training.

COMPENSATION

The sum of money awarded to the victor in any claims heard by an INDUSTRIAL TRIBUNAL. The amount is either prescribed by legislation or established by case law applying to a comparable situation. In law courts compensation is referred to as DAMAGES.

In US, and now many UK companies, compensation means the cash element of the total reward package. It is sometimes used interchangeably with REMUNERATION to mean PAY including BENEFITS.

COMPETENCY

The knowledge, skills and personal qualities needed to do something, and how those attributes are applied. The emphasis in competency models is on *how* things are done, not on *what* has to be produced. For example, a sales representative will need a knowledge of the product and the market, numerical skills and the power of persuasion. Competencies are increasingly being used by organisations to assess potential employees at the RECRUITMENT stage, and also in the APPRAISAL, training and DEVELOPMENT of existing employees.

In the UK the competency approach is being encouraged by the National Vocational Qualification (NVQ) system and, through its use, by a number of professional bodies. In the USA many people believe that by identifying management competencies, organisations can improve management performance by designing recruitment and training approaches that measure and develop the specified competencies. The European Commission is keen for competencies to be used throughout the European Union, as all EU citizens can work in any member state. Using competencies helps get over the problem that the same job title may mean different things in different countries, although the same could of course be true of competencies.

At the management level competencies are considered to be groups of skills, knowledge, values and personal attributes, such as adaptability, integrity, decisivemess, project planning, innovation and people management. Some competencies, such as adaptability, are more easily understood as inputs, whereas others, such as innovation, are more readily measured as outputs. An example of a definition of innovation might be: having the ability to construct new radical alternatives to traditional working methods and approaches.

Once it starts to be impersonal, it's time to break up the company.
Richard Branson

COMPETITION BY EX-EMPLOYEES

It is not unusual for ex-employees to set up in competition with their former employer. This can be irritating and potentially damaging to the former employer. Obviously, SELF-EMPLOYED staff are free, through the nature of their relationship with an employer, to work for rivals.

Ex-employees, even those who have left on good terms through early retirement or voluntary REDUNDANCY or for a new job, can cause harm to a former employer by using information or contacts obtained in a previous job. This also happens in the public sector, where ex-employees often move into consultancies. An employer can anticipate the problem by insisting on a "no-competition" or "restraint of trade" clause in the CONTRACT OF EMPLOYMENT. This can specify the activities, the period of time and the geographical area covered. Typically, a skilled employee, such as a research chemist, marketing manager or insurance agent, can be stopped from setting up in business in competition, providing it is reasonable and in the public interest to do so.

The public interest is generally considered to be served by the existence of as many services and products as possible. However, the LAW sees the need to balance this interest with that of the employer who trained, developed and provided opportunities for the employee in question. It is therefore sensible to draft a clause that clearly specifies the banned activities, such as approaching clients or using mailing lists or other material, and then set reasonable restrictions. In terms of time this is normally 1–2 years. The restricted area will depend on the business; the more specialised and sophisticated it is the more the law will accept the need for wide geographical protection. For example, it would not be reasonable to prevent a car mechanic from obtaining employment "anywhere in the European Union", whereas a worldwide restriction might be appropriate if the ex-employee had a crucial research role in developing a preventative drug for AIDS.

CONFIDENTIAL INFORMATION

People often say that issues are confidential when all they want to do is keep decisions or information to themselves. You can write "confidential" on letters or documents simply to indicate restricted access, but if someone given such confidential information discloses it to an unauthorised person, the legal remedy is uncertain because there is no clear definition of the word. However, if you indicate that a topic is confidential and the LAW considers such a label appropriate because the information relates, for example, to strategic plans, discussions about pay or promotion or technical data, you can seek an INJUNCTION to restrain the use of the data or claim damages, especially if the data have already been used improperly.

Employers should be clear about what can be properly classified as confidential and should communicate that fact to employees together with the consequences of divulging such information.

CONSTRUCTIVE DISMISSAL
When employees leave a job because they rightly consider their position has been made untenable under the terms of their contract. For example, they have been expected to continue to work in unsafe conditions that have been drawn to their employer's attention. In the UK such employees can then claim for UNFAIR DISMISSAL or a REDUNDANCY payment. In a case of constructive dismissal the employer must have broken an express term of the CONTRACT OF EMPLOYMENT (such as failing to pay WAGES or forcing an employee to change agreed hours of work) or an implied term (such as the right of the employee not to be harassed or bullied). In short, to successfully claim constructive dismissal, employees must show that the damage caused by the employer to the employment relationship is so great that they cannot carry on working.

CONSULTANTS
See OUTSOURCING; EMPLOYMENT STATUS; FLEXIBLE WORKFORCE.

CONSULTATION

To consult means to take counsel, to ask advice and to seek opinion. The word has entered the workplace both through industrial relations legislation and from a changing attitude to the management of staff. Consultation, whether formal or informal, means that the company is seeking the opinions of its staff about aspects of the workplace that will affect them.

Throughout most of Europe there are statutory obligations for employers to consult elected employee REPRESENTATIVES at corporate and workplace level before taking decisions that affect the organisation of the business and the day-to-day conduct of personnel management. Exactly which issues must be the subject of consultation, and the extent of other rights to information and participation in decision-making, vary considerably among countries. In some countries, most notably Germany and the Netherlands, an employer often cannot act without the consent of employee representatives (see MITBESTIMMUNG). Although this often slows down the pace of decision-making to a speed that a UK- or US-based employer might find irksome, it does serve to create a broader basis of legitimacy for a course of action once decided on.

EU directives oblige employers to consult with elected employee representatives or representatives of recognised trade unions when redundancies or a transfer of the whole or parts of a business are proposed. Moreover, companies must provide in their annual reports details of any actions taken to improve communication and consultation with their workforces.

Legislation following the EU SOCIAL CHAPTER also requires large employers operating across European boundaries to set up bodies (usually referred to as works councils) for employee information and consultation at the European level. The European Commission has also raised the possibility of legislating for consultation in smaller companies which do not have substantial cross-border employment.

The effectiveness of consultation depends on

the extent to which senior management are willing to share information, and whether employees believe they have the opportunity to contribute their opinions. A variety of methods can be used, including:

- TEAM BRIEFINGS;
- QUALITY CIRCLEs;
- departmental meetings;
- joint consultative committees.

CONTINUING PROFESSIONAL DEVELOPMENT

An increasing number of professional institutions around the world are encouraging their members to keep up to date with developments in their area of expertise. Student members may have to keep a work book detailing their experience and courses they have attended, which can be inspected by examiners and tutors. In many countries this is a requirement for students taking professional accountancy exams. Some institutions may make the upgrading or continuation of membership conditional on the submission of a professional development record detailing how individuals have kept up to date and improved their professional knowledge.

CONTINUITY

Employees who know their rights may ask each other: "What is your continuity?" This is because, traditionally, statutory employment rights apply only after a set period of CONTINUOUS EMPLOYMENT, for example two years for a REDUNDANCY claim. This generally applies throughout Europe and the USA, although the periods may differ. There are obvious attractions for employers to break an employee's continuity of employment, especially where work is uncertain or there are economic pressures. However, the following should be borne in mind.

- Employees have continuity for as long as their CONTRACT OF EMPLOYMENT exists, for example through ILLNESS, statutory maternity

leave, SECONDMENT, HOLIDAY or by the payment of a retainer.
- Where a contract ends and is then renewed (as it often is in agriculture, fishing, construction, catering and home working), the break will not interrupt continuity if it is a temporary cessation or there is an occupational custom that assumes the employment relationship is ongoing. Breaks are temporary in LAW if they are shorter than periods in work when considered on an annual basis, providing there is a mutual expectation that when work is available again it will be offered to and accepted by the employee. This legal process can ensure that, ironically, casual workers can have long periods of continuity and may thus be entitled to COMPENSATION when the arrangement finally ends.
- Continuity is preserved in the case of something covered by TUPE or when staff are transferred to an associated employer. It can be also preserved by legislation affecting the public sector or, of course, by employers who voluntarily recognise interrupted periods of employment as continuous.

CONTINUOUS EMPLOYMENT
Most of your rights as an employee depend upon how long you have worked for an employer (see CONTINUITY above).

CONTINUOUS IMPROVEMENT
See *KAIZEN*.

CONTRACT OF EMPLOYMENT
The legally binding agreement between an employer and an employee governing their mutual obligations. It should use appropriate language and be signed by both parties. A contract's terms override any other evidence, such as CUSTOM AND PRACTICE, but any terms in a contract that purport to override the employee's common law or statutory employment rights is null and void. The writ-

ten STATEMENT OF TERMS OF WORK required by the Employment Rights Act 1996 is not a contract of employment but it does provide evidence of the terms of a contract. It may be overridden by other evidence. It is estimated that around 40% of employers believe they are using binding written contracts of employment when they are actually using statements of terms.

The contract or statement should contain the following information:

- Name and address of employer and normal PLACE OF WORK (if it differs from the address)
- Name of employee
- Job title
- Date of appointment
- PAY, payment interval, method of payment, normal payment date
- HOURS OF WORK
- HOLIDAY offered, including public holidays
- Length of contract

Optional information which can be in the contract or available to the employee in, say, the STAFF HANDBOOK includes the following:

- Confidentiality
- COPYRIGHT and INTELLECTUAL PROPERTY rights
- Disciplinary rules and procedures
- Driving licence inspection
- EXPENSES while on company business
- GRIEVANCE PROCEDURE
- HEALTH AND SAFETY policy
- Hygiene rules
- No-smoking rules
- NOTICE period
- Notifying employer of other employment
- Other benefits
- Pension arrangements
- Pregnancy notification
- Restrictions on future competitive activity
- Right of search
- Security of company property
- SICK PAY procedures and entitlements

- Undertaking other commensurate duties
- Uniform requirements

CONTRACT STAFF

Staff employed on a contract are usually skilled, SELF-EMPLOYED workers. The label "contract" means much the same as freelance. Whether it is legally convincing as self-employment is another matter (see EMPLOYMENT STATUS). Employing staff on a contract basis has advantages for organisations, allowing them to meet short-term demand and probably avoid statutory obligations to employees, such as SICK PAY. However, if a contract worker is inefficient, alienates customers or other employees, or produces shoddy work, the only control an employer has is to end the contract (as opposed to disciplining an employee), which can be complicated and acrimonious. The short-term gains of employing people on contract may be at the expense of such things as consistency, continuity and business reputation. Contract workers will be loyal to themselves or their profession, but not necessarily to you.

Employment contracts? They are surely simply a way of transmitting the will of the employer.
Managing director, electronics company, 1995

COPYRIGHT

An INTELLECTUAL PROPERTY right in, for example, a report, a piece of software or an advertising jingle, which is written down or displayed graphically. It is often a valuable asset.

Organisations that commission outsiders to prepare reports, develop products and so on should consider the copyright implications and ensure that the agreement specifies who owns the copyright. If they do not, the presumption will be that the copyright remains with the outsider as the "creator" of the work.

CORPORATE CULTURE

A commonly held set of assumptions about an organisation's values and behaviours. Edgar Schein, who helped develop the concept, believes that the key to successful LEADERSHIP is managing cultural change and outlined five key areas in which this consensus should operate.

1 The Mission: what business are we in, and why?
2 The goals, to include specific goals for all.
3 The means to accomplish the goals, including the reward systems.
4 The means of measuring progress with feedback.
5 The strategies for what to do when things go wrong.

Following the motivational theories of Abraham Maslow, Frederick Herzberg, Chris Argyris and Douglas McGregor, his MENTOR at MIT, Schein set out to discover what creates motivation. Why, for example, do millionaires persist in seeking more millions and constantly set themselves new and more difficult goals?

COVENANT
See RESTRAINT OF TRADE CLAUSE.

CRIMINAL ACTS
Some criminal acts can be concerned with work, such as embezzlement, fraud and VIOLENCE. These will probably be covered by disciplinary rules as well as criminal law. If an employee is accused of a crime that took place outside work an employer may not want to take any action in the case of, say, a motoring offence, an offence under the Dangerous Dogs Act, or a petty THEFT. However, an offence of violence, fraud or one that attracts publicity may need careful consideration.

Tribunals and courts are generally sympathetic to the need of employers to protect their reputations. Suspension of the employee until the court case is resolved is often a useful option, but it must be handled sensitively. Employees should be told the reason for the suspension and its likely length. They should be paid during the suspension, and the process should be carefully documented. An employer can, of course, dismiss an employee for acts of serious violence or gross dishonesty, subject to the organisation's DISCIPLINARY PROCEDURE.

If an employee is found guilty and sent to prison, an employer can probably end his or her contract on the ground of CAPABILITY, because they cannot work and be in prison at the same time. Even if the employee is released following an appeal, his or her DISMISSAL will probably be justified. There is a business to run and the facts had to be judged at the relevant time.

CUSTOM AND PRACTICE

A way of formulating the rules that govern employment. A custom does not have force because it has been specifically prescribed but because it has come to be accepted. Terms of a CONTRACT OF EMPLOYMENT may be implied through custom and practice where, over a period of time, they have regularly applied. For example, if management have provided all employees with an extra day off at Christmas for the last ten years, it is likely to be seen as a contractual entitlement.

Custom and practice is not static. It develops to suit the needs of employers and employees. Trade unions seek not only to protect the principle of custom, but also to develop it to give greater security to their members. The wider use of formal, explicit agreements and procedures has not put an end to custom and practice. Jobs cannot be totally specified, and reliance on custom is important for filling in the gaps, as well as for keeping agreements simple.

D

DAMAGES

The sum of money you have to pay when it all goes wrong. Damages are awarded by courts (it is called COMPENSATION in an INDUSTRIAL TRIBUNAL) when, for example, an employee is injured by an employer's negligence. Damages are assessed so as to replace loss of earnings, both past and future, and cover medical and other costs. There are going rates for most injuries, for example, for loss of an eye or STRESS. They are usually possible to predict.

DATA ON EMPLOYEES

A lot of data on employees, covering, for example, personnel, medical and training matters, is held by employers on paper or as computer files. Most data should be treated as CONFIDENTIAL INFORMATION and kept in locked filing cabinets or secure electronic locations. Concern about the use of such data has led governments to introduce legislation to govern access to it and disclosure of it.

In the UK the Data Protection Act 1984 imposes obligations on employers who hold data and gives rights to employees to whom the data relate. Companies keeping data on computer must register with the Data Protection Registrar. Failure to do so is a criminal offence. There is no obligation, however, for the holders of data to tell people that their personal data are being held unless the data subject asks. It is nevertheless good practice for personal data held on an employer's computerised system to be printed out and sent to its employees so they can check it. The printout may contain a statement for the employee to sign, confirming that the record is accurate, or that it requires amendment.

The European Union's Directive on the Protection of Personal Data, due to be implemented at national level in 1999, will provide an overarching framework complementing existing national legislation, requiring changes in some instances and creating a platform for the exchange of personal data across national borders. This will make it easier, for example, for multinational employers to transfer data on their employees between national locations. It will apply to manual records as well as computerised ones. Some data relating, for example, to health, RELIGION and SEXUAL ORIENTATION can only be recorded and transmitted with the consent of the employee concerned.

DATE OF TERMINATION

The agreed date that the employment ceases of someone who has resigned, been fired or been made redundant. It should always be put in writing, either as part of the formal NOTICE of DISMISSAL or REDUNDANCY, or in the letter accepting someone's RESIGNATION. If an employer does not want an employee to work until the end of the notice period, the company rules or CONTRACT OF EMPLOYMENT should, in theory, state that the employer can terminate the contract at an earlier date than the expiry of notice, and that the company will offer PAY in lieu. In practice, most people are happy to accept an offer of pay in lieu whatever their contract says.

DEATH

When an employee dies the CONTRACT OF EMPLOYMENT ends, but any unsettled claim against the employer is not affected. Any money or COMPENSATION due goes to the former employee's estate.

DECENTRALISATION

Devolving substantial amounts of management power and accountability away from the corporate centre to semi-autonomous divisions or business units. The concept was put into practice by Alfred Sloan at General Motors in the 1920s. Alfred Chandler, an economic historian at Harvard in the 1940s, was the first management writer to recognise the importance of decentralisation to corporations which had become large, unwieldy and stultified, when he was researching the relationship between strategy and structure. Peter Drucker has also described decentralisation as one of the key management planks for business success.

DEDUCTIONS FROM PAY

An employer can deduct money from an employee's WAGES only if the LAW allows or the employee consents. Under the UK Employment Rights Act 1996 no employer can make deductions from wages, receive payment from a worker, or fail to pay wages due to a worker unless authorisation is provided:

- by the worker in writing; or
- by a statutory provision; or
- by a relevant provision in the CONTRACT OF EMPLOYMENT.

Excluded from this, however, are deductions and payments made:

- on account of an employee's participation in a strike or other INDUSTRIAL ACTION;
- to reimburse the employer for overpayment of wages or expenses;
- as a consequence of a DISCIPLINARY PROCEDURE;
- where there is a requirement under a statutory provision to deduct and pay specified amounts, such as PAYE and NATIONAL INSURANCE;
- to a third party in accordance with arrangements detailed in the employee's contract, or authorised by prior agreement, or covered by a court order such as ATTACHMENT OF EARNINGS;
- where the worker has provided written consent to comply wholly or partly with a court order or tribunal that requires payment of a specified amount to the employer.

DELAYERING

With a better-educated workforce the devolution of responsibility down the hierarchical structure of the organisation through EMPOWERMENT has meant that many middle management levels have become superfluous. This delayering of the hierarchy has led to the current flatter organisation structures of the 1990s.

> *Delayering can be defined as the process by which people who barely know what's going on get rid of those people that do.*
> Henry Mintzberg

DETRIMENT

A word used to describe any loss or disadvantage to an employee. It covers failing to obtain or losing a job, not being promoted, being suspended from work or being otherwise sidelined. It can form the basis of an INDUSTRIAL TRIBUNAL claim, for example, where an employee who has blown the whistle on illegal HEALTH AND SAFETY or DISCRIMINATION practices is later fired or sidelined.

DIGNITY AT WORK

The concept that employees should be treated properly regardless of sex, RACE, AGE, DISABILITY, SEXUAL ORIENTATION, and so on. The European Union's 1991 Recommendation on Dignity at Work views dignity as a generic right for all employees. It contains a Code of Practice which can be applied in, or adapted to suit, all workplaces. It identifies the key personnel practices, such as training, providing information, consultation and discipline, which are needed to ensure dignity. The Recommendation cannot be used directly by alleged "victims", but it is a practical benchmark used in courts and tribunals throughout the EU.

DIRECTOR

A private company must have at least one director, who, whatever their title, is responsible for management. A public company must have a minimum of two directors. A director is a company officer, and may also be an employee. An employee director is entitled to the same protection as other employees against REDUNDANCY and UNFAIR DISMISSAL.

DISABILITY

Many countries have legislation that outlaws DISCRIMINATION against disabled people. In the UK the Disability Discrimination Act 1995, which came into force on December 2nd 1996, makes it unlawful to discriminate unfairly against both physically and mentally disabled people. The act highlights RECRUITMENT and employment criteria, but exempts companies with fewer than 20 employees. Individuals who think they have been unfairly discriminated against have the right to take their complaint to an INDUSTRIAL TRIBUNAL. There is no limit on the amount a tribunal can award.

In recruitment, it is unlawful to discriminate against a disabled person in arrangements for determining who will be employed, in the terms on which employment is offered, or by refusing or deliberately not offering employment. Once a disabled person is employed, it is unlawful to discriminate against them in opportunities for promotion, transfer, training or any other BENEFITS, including OCCUPATIONAL PENSION schemes. The act also requires employers to make reasonable adjustments to working hours, conditions or the workplace where this will help to overcome the practical effects of a person's disability. A disabled applicant who is not shortlisted for a post can challenge the decision under the Disability Discrimination Act. If this happens the employer should prepare a response to the following questions.

- Why can the applicant not perform the job?
- If there are problems, could they be overcome by adjustments, such as different equipment, HOMEWORKING or JOB SHARING?
- Could additional training and support help to make the job feasible?

If the firm is small and the cost of making adaptations is considerable, the decision not to offer a job might be defensible. However, the options would still need to be explored and the reasons must be presented with TRANSPARENCY.

Organisations are affected by the act in other

ways. For example, it is unlawful for a provider of services, whether paid for or not, to refuse services or to offer them on different terms to a disabled person. A number of European countries have legislation requiring employers to ensure that a given proportion of their workforce are registered disabled people, with fines or penalties for those who fail to meet their quota. In Italy the quota is as high as 15%. Grants are available in many countries to adapt workplaces for use by disabled people.

DISABILITY WORKING ALLOWANCE

A disabled person working 16 or more hours a week cannot claim the JOBSEEKER'S ALLOWANCE or certain other benefits. Disability working allowance is a tax-free cash benefit paid to ensure that disabled people are no worse off working than if they were unemployed.

DISCIPLINARY PROCEDURE

A formal procedure laid down by an organisation to deal with MISCONDUCT by employees. All staff need to be fully aware of the type of behaviour their company defines as misconduct and what the disciplinary procedures are. If there is a STAFF HANDBOOK, the details are likely to be listed there, together with grievance procedures. When formulating a policy it is sensible for employers to take advice on what other organisations do. In the UK the ACAS Code of Practice offers guidance on setting up and operating disciplinary procedures.

DISCIPLINE AT WORK

Employees are expected to behave themselves at work, produce work of a satisfactory standard and conduct themselves in a reasonable manner. This is an unwritten yet implied term in their CONTRACT OF EMPLOYMENT. Employees who misbehave can be disciplined, but unless the misconduct is deemed to be serious they may not have breached their contracts. If more than 20 people are employed there must be disciplinary rules and procedures to advise them how to complain about a disciplinary decision, how to air a grievance and how to proceed with the complaint. The most serious form of discipline is DISMISSAL. Others include oral warnings, written warnings, SUSPENSION FROM WORK, fines and demotion.

DISCRIMINATION
People are protected by LAW against being unfairly treated on account of their RACE, skin colour, RELIGION, nationality, gender, marital status or DISABILITY. But employers can discriminate on the ground of AGE. (See also SEXUAL DISCRIMINATION.)

DISMISSAL
When an employer terminates a CONTRACT OF EMPLOYMENT, with or without NOTICE, it is known as dismissal. Failure to renew a FIXED-TERM contract within four weeks of its termination is also a dismissal for REDUNDANCY.

The employer must follow a fair procedure or the employee may claim UNFAIR DISMISSAL. If the dismissal is without notice (often called summary dismissal) the employee may claim WRONGFUL DISMISSAL, except where he or she is guilty of gross misconduct or gross NEGLIGENCE. If the employer commits a serious BREACH OF CONTRACT which drives the employee to resign, the employee may claim CONSTRUCTIVE DISMISSAL.

DISPLAY SCREEN EQUIPMENT
The screens in front of which so many people now spend a large part of their working lives have given rise to numerous health worries over the years. In the UK the Health and Safety (Display Screen Equipment) Regulations 1992, which came into force on January 1st 1993, generated a thriving service industry of organisations offering to carry out risk-assessment exercises and test equipment and furniture covered by the regulations (most of which organisations can and should do for themselves). Based on an EU directive, the UK legislation was a watered-down interpretation of more stringent regulations already in force in Germany and Sweden. The display screen equipment

(DSE) regulations require the "systematic and considered application of established good practice". They relate to "workers who habitually use display screens for a significant part of their normal work". Employers are obliged to:

- carry out an analysis of workstations to assess and reduce risks, for example, the provision of sufficient workspace, display screens with brightness and contrast controls, and adjustable viewing, keyboard and seating positions. The elbows should be in the same horizontal plane as the middle row of the keyboard and the eyes a minimum of 38cm away from the screen;
- plan workloads to provide breaks;
- ensure eyesight protection, and provide eyesight tests and special spectacles if required;
- provide HEALTH AND SAFETY training for all individuals;
- provide information and consultation to the workforce.
- be alert to any employees that might be concerned about radiation, such as pregnant women.

The 1992 regulations applied immediately to new workstations, but employers had until January 1st 1997 to modify existing workstations. Non-adjustable chairs are likely to fail the regulation that users must "be able to find a comfortable seating position".

Fatigue from intensive DSE work can cause discomfort but there are no indications, despite extensive research, that it causes permanent eye damage, although headaches can be generated by a poor DSE image quality, a flickering screen, glare and poor posture. However, worries about radiation seem to have been quashed by research indicating that people probably receive a larger dose of radiation each time they open their microwaves than from a year in front of DSE.

DOWNSIZING

A euphemism for slashing employee numbers that came into vogue when recession hit in the 1980s. Downsizing was a simple way to cut costs and was often justified by management, at least in part, on the ground of improvements in new technology. Now that firms have rediscovered the attraction of holding on to skilled staff and of a high-morale workforce that feels secure, it is products that are being downsized. With greater environmental awareness among consumers, companies (notably those in the automobile industry) have been grasping the opportunities that lie in making and marketing smaller things.

> *Not many organisations can survive on cost cutting alone. Those which survive in the long term are those which have not done the most appalling things to their employees.*
> Paul Herriot, 1997

DRESS

Codes of dress have changed dramatically throughout the world in the last ten years. Formality has become less important, as recognised by the increasing implementation by companies of a policy that allows employees to "dress-down" on Fridays. But in many organisations the corporate culture and image employees present requires certain standards of dress, even uniforms.

DRUGS

Workplace policies on the misuse of drugs are still rare. However, legislation and growing public concern have encouraged employers, especially in high-risk areas, to introduce policies to address the issues of poor performance, ABSENCE and accidents caused by the use of drugs.

The main reason for introducing a policy on drugs is safety, for the company's employees and those that could be affected by accidents or poor performance. Under HEALTH AND SAFETY legislation in developed countries employers have a DUTY OF

CARE to provide a safe working environment. In some instances there is legislation that specifically deals with drugs use at work. For example, in the UK the Transport and Works Act 1992 makes it illegal for transport workers in safety-sensitive positions to report for duty after drinking ALCOHOL or taking drugs.

An employer can test employees for drugs, but such a procedure is rare in most industries (with the exception of transport). If employees consent, testing can take place at the RECRUITMENT stage and random tests may be carried out during employment. Some employers treat drugs use as a health problem, whereas others see it as a disciplinary issue. Employees who are high on drugs can be dismissed if their performance or behaviour at work is affected; it is not generally necessary for there to be specific rules permitting dismissal for using illegal drugs during working hours. Employees who use drugs outside work put themselves at risk of disciplinary action if their performance at work causes problems.

DSE
See DISPLAY SCREEN EQUIPMENT.

DUTY OF CARE
All employees and others working for an organisation and people affected by its operations (for example, those who live nearby) are owed a duty of care. If someone suffers injury or loss as a result of activities an organisation should have foreseen might cause such injury or loss, the organisation is in breach of its duty of care and will have to pay compensation (DAMAGES). The yardstick of how much care should be taken is, generally, "reasonable". The definition of reasonable care is ultimately a matter for the courts, but it is not a sufficient defence for employers to say they did not know about likely risks or of practical ways to deal with them. Information and advice on, for example, dealing with noise and STRESS, making machines safe, lifting loads safely or using DISPLAY SCREEN EQUIPMENT are widely and often cheaply

available. The LAW does not allow companies to turn a blind eye or argue that the duty of care is too expensive to comply with.

Employers should recognise that the duty of care is also owed to non-employees such as customers, clients, casual workers and the general public. It is also important to note that the standards expected of employers are constantly rising (see HEALTH AND SAFETY).

E

EAP
See EMPLOYEE ASSISTANCE PROGRAMMES.

ECJ
See EUROPEAN COURT OF JUSTICE.

EMPLOYED PERSON
An individual who works for someone under a CONTRACT OF EMPLOYMENT and is covered by EMPLOYMENT PROTECTION legislation.

EMPLOYEE ASSISTANCE PROGRAMMES
In the past employees with personal problems were often left to stew in their own anxieties. Today they may be helped through employee assistance programmes (EAPs), which are offered by employers who have realised that STRESS affects individual performance and may lead to genuine sickness ABSENCE. Many organisations provide free external, confidential counselling services, generally through a 24-hour telephone helpline, for employees with problems related to work, family, money, and so on. Once the underlying cause of the problem is diagnosed, more expert advice can be offered.

EAPs first appeared in the USA in response to the high incidence of employee alcoholism, which was reported to be costing industry some $40bn per year. Over 2 million American employees now use such services each year. EAPs are also becoming popular in the UK, with an estimated 5% of the workforce now offered the service. The ultimate aim of the service provider is that resolution of the problem should lead to improved employee performance. There is still debate, however, about the effect of these programmes, in respect of their expense and the fact that, because they are confidential, they do not get to grips with the organisational (as opposed to individual) causes of stress.

EMPLOYEE OPINION SURVEY
A survey used by a company to find out what staff think about its performance, PAY, BENEFITS and

conditions of employment, management style, and so on. The surveys are strictly confidential, and are usually conducted by external agencies.

The only place where success comes before work is in the dictionary.
Vidal Sassoon

EMPLOYEES' STATUTORY RIGHTS

The major rights of employees enshrined in LAW in the UK and throughout the European Union relate to job security, EQUAL OPPORTUNITY and HEALTH AND SAFETY. An increasing number of them, for example the right to opt out of Sunday working, are applicable regardless of length of service or weekly hours of work. Legislation prevents employers from doing deals with employees not to exercise their statutory rights. For example, a document signed by an employee saying "I agree that if there is a downturn in work and the company faces financial difficulties I will have to leave and will not burden the company with a redundancy claim" will be ignored by an INDUSTRIAL TRIBUNAL.

In the UK the major statutory rights are included in the Employment Rights Act 1996, although other legislation covers DISCRIMINATION and HEALTH AND SAFETY. They include the right:

- to a written STATEMENT OF TERMS OF WORK and itemised PAY statements;
- not to have DEDUCTIONS FROM PAY without prior written consent;
- to EQUAL PAY and equal opportunities for men and women, members of an ETHNIC MINORITY or those suffering a DISABILITY;
- to have paid or unpaid (depending on the right) time off from work in certain circumstances, such as for antenatal appointments;
- not to be victimised at work for bringing INDUSTRIAL TRIBUNAL cases or whistle-blowing on health and safety;

- to minimum NOTICE periods;
- not to be unfairly dismissed or made REDUNDANT without COMPENSATION.

There is currently no statutory right to minimum pay. Some groups of workers, especially those on short contracts, are unable to exercise all the rights listed above.

EMPLOYERS' LIABILITY

Employers are liable for any civil wrongs committed by their employees in the normal course of employment. Anyone who suffers loss as a result may be able to recover DAMAGES from the employer.

EMPLOYMENT AGENCY

An organisation that helps someone to find a job or an employer to fill a vacancy. Employment agencies are controlled by LAW to protect the people who use them, and in the UK come under the jurisdiction of the Department of Trade and Industry. It is illegal for agencies to charge fees to people looking for jobs, apart from models and actors. They can charge employers as much as they like.

EMPLOYMENT APPEAL TRIBUNAL

A UK tribunal that hears appeals from an INDUSTRIAL TRIBUNAL. It has a lawyer as chairman, usually a High Court judge, and two lay members. It can decide only on matters of LAW, that is, whether legislation or case law was properly applied to the facts in the original hearing. It cannot revisit the facts. Further appeals can be made by the loser to the Court of Appeal (Court of Session in Scotland) and then to the House of Lords.

EMPLOYMENT AT WILL

The US common law doctrine that protects an employer's right to discharge workers for good, bad or no reason at all. There are laws that protect certain categories of employees. For example, the Civil Rights Act 1972 protects private- and public-sector employees from unjust DISMISSAL based on RACE, RELIGION, sex or national origin.

EMPLOYMENT PROTECTION
The Employment Rights Act 1996 and the Employment Protection (Part-time Employees) Regulations 1995 entitle UK employees to be treated fairly at work and if they lose their jobs. Qualifying periods for employment rights are clearly set out.

EMPLOYMENT STATUS
This is one of the most complex issues facing employers. An organisation may employ casual workers, freelancers, consultants, CONTRACT STAFF and so on, and it is crucial to get their employment status right. If individuals are employees rather than SELF-EMPLOYED there are practical implications for employers.

- Tax and NATIONAL INSURANCE contributions must be deducted from their earnings through PAYE.
- They must be insured against an occupational injury or ill health.
- Their statutory employment rights must be recognised.
- Employers are liable for any injury, loss or damage their employees may cause to others in the course of their employment.

There are some obvious attractions in employing people on a self-employed basis, although they still enjoy statutory rights such as those banning DISCRIMINATION and they are owed a DUTY OF CARE. However, it is the nature of the employment rather than the employer's decision that determines someone's employment status.

To protect themselves, employers can seek advice on someone's employment status from the Inland Revenue and specialist inspectors or from a lawyer, accountant or business adviser. However, research has shown that such advice is not always correct and may be rejected by a court.

The basic question in determining employment status is whether individuals are in business on their own account. In other words, do they provide their own equipment, decide substantially when and how work is done, fix a fee for the work and, most importantly, work for other people? If they do, then such individuals are likely to be genuinely self-employed. That someone only works a few hours for an organisation or their income falls below the tax threshold does not mean they are not an employee.

EMPOWERMENT

The process of devolving responsibility and authority for planning and decision-making down an organisation's hierarchy. The DELAYERING in companies around the world may have removed large chunks of middle management, but many of its functions still need to be carried out, hence the evolution of the concept of empowerment. When asked, most people will suggest that they are not being used to their full potential. By empowering them companies can help managers cope with the responsibility of dealing with day-to-day operations as well as the task of planning for the future. Most people are capable of doing more; they just need some training, some COACHING when they ask for it and lots of encouragement (without having to ask for it). Empowerment is not an easy option. It should not be embarked upon until employees have the skills and competencies to deal with, and are ready and willing to take on, new tasks and responsibilities.

> *Control does not cease with empowerment. It is stronger, since it is being exercised by everyone.*
> Rosabeth Moss Kanter

EQUAL OPPORTUNITY

Legislation that makes SEXUAL DISCRIMINATION unlawful is common throughout the industrialised world. The USA led the way with comprehensive federal laws. In the UK the Equal Opportunities

Commission was set up in 1975 to work to remove unlawful DISCRIMINATION on the grounds of sex or marital status and to promote equal opportunities for women and men. It can help people who are making claims under EQUAL PAY legislation, and has powers to investigate discriminatory practices and take action to gain compliance with the legislation. The commission recommends that organisations should:

- let their employees know that they are an equal opportunities employer;
- include an equal opportunities statement in all job advertisements;
- recruit from all sections of the community;
- ensure that all staff have equal access to training and development opportunities;
- consider flexible working arrangements such as PART-TIME WORK, JOB SHARING, flexible working hours, working from home and fixed-term contracts for specific projects;
- provide a clear and simple complaints procedure, and make sure that it covers the possibility of HARASSMENT;
- review regularly how its equal opportunities policy is working.

If the language requirements in a job specification are essential in order to carry out the normal duties of the job, the specification in a job description or recruitment advertisement will not infringe equal opportunities legislation.

EQUAL PAY

The principle that individuals who do equivalent jobs should be paid the same, regardless of their sex, is still less widely applied than it should be. Equal pay was awarded to women civil servants in the USA in 1870, and by 1955 it had been introduced by 16 other countries. Article 119 of the Treaty of Rome states that each member of the European Economic Community (now the European Union) should apply the principle of equal REMUNERATION for equal work for men and women.

This has now progressed from equal work to work of equal value.

But what is work of equal value? If two jobs have been evaluated without any sexual bias, using a JOB EVALUATION scheme, this will be seen as providing the required evidence. If there has been no evaluation, the jobs will be reviewed, taking into account such factors as effort, skills and decision-making, as well as others that appear to be significant.

Progress on equal pay in Europe has been mixed. In the Netherlands, for example, a national job evaluation scheme has made it fairly easy to establish work of equal value. In France and Italy equal pay legislation has been in place since 1945 and 1947 respectively. All EU member states, irrespective of their own domestic legislation, are subject to the two equal pay and EQUAL OPPORTUNITY directives passed in the mid-1970s. The principles embodied in the Treaty of Rome have been developed by the EUROPEAN COURT OF JUSTICE through clarification of the concept of pay to include PENSIONS (and pension ages).

In the UK equal pay legislation applies to employees of all ages, as well as part-time and full-time workers, temporary and permanent workers, homeworkers, contractors and apprentices. The Equal Pay Act 1970 states that a woman is entitled to equal pay with a man who is "in the same employment". The act defines this as being employed by the same employer, or any associated employer, at the same establishment, or at establishments in the UK which include the one in question, and where there are common terms and conditions of employment for the group of employees being considered. This means that men and women must be treated equally in terms of pay and BENEFITS, if they are employed in "like work", work rated as equivalent under a job evaluation scheme, or work judged to be of equal value.

Equal pay claims can cut across different occupational groups, and jobs may be compared which are quite dissimilar in nature, for example, a cook with a painter. In the event of an equal pay claim, the onus is on the employer to prove that the job evaluation methodology it has used has no sexual bias. Both parties to the case may call "expert witnesses", who are recognised experts in job evaluation, to assist with their cases.

ERGONOMICS

The application of human physiological science to the workplace. Ergonomics was popular in the 1960s and 1970s, especially in the Nordic countries, the UK and the USA. Interest in it has revived, largely because of the rise in problems associated with using DISPLAY SCREEN EQUIPMENT and awareness of the huge incidence and cost of back injuries at work. Ergonomists argue that conditions such as REPETITIVE STRAIN INJURY, carpel tunnel syndrome and "tennis elbow" are not caused by work equipment itself but by poor posture, poor support and, importantly, long, unbroken working hours. European HEALTH AND SAFETY legislation requires that work must be fitted to the individual, not the other way round.

ETHNIC MINORITY

Research continues to show that some ethnic groups suffer disproportionately high unemployment rates and are less likely to hold senior jobs in organisations. In the UK RACE relations legislation applies to racial and ethnic groups (but not religious groups other than in Northern Ireland and not to political beliefs) and takes its lead from the USA.

Measures employers can take to minimise ethnic disadvantage include ethnic monitoring and racial awareness programmes. They should also take care with all RECRUITMENT, selection and promotion processes to avoid racial bias. Even some of the most well established psychometric tests have been criticised on this ground. Much advice is available from professional and governmental organisations.

EUROPEAN COURT OF HUMAN RIGHTS

Based in Strasbourg, the European Court of

Human Rights considers whether members of the European Convention of Human Rights have broken the rules. Governments are not obliged to act as a result of its findings but the embarrassment factor provides a strong incentive for them to do so. Well publicised cases have concerned corporal punishment, wire-tapping, treatment of prisoners, transsexuals' rights at work and TRADE UNION rights.

EUROPEAN COURT OF JUSTICE

The European Court of Justice (ECJ) is based in Luxembourg and its main role is to interpret the treaties and other legislation of the European Union. Its legal decisions are final and binding on member states. It includes judges from all the member states and cases are referred from the national courts or brought by individuals. It is gradually shaping European employment LAW, especially in areas of EQUAL OPPORTUNITY, rights to TIME OFF, MATERNITY RIGHTS, WORKING TIME, aspects of job security and HEALTH AND SAFETY.

The ECJ has exercised an especially influential role through important judgements on the interpretation of the Treaty of Rome and directives on EQUAL PAY, with important ramifications for pension rights and RETIREMENT ages, and in the field of the TRANSFER OF UNDERTAKINGS. In particular, the ECJ has been instrumental in developing the notion of indirect DISCRIMINATION, a situation where unequal treatment of employees of a particular type, such as part-timers, can be forbidden because these employees are mainly or wholly women.

EUROPEAN LAW

The legal rules of the European Union which take precedence over equivalent national laws. EU legislation derives its ultimate force from the various treaties signed by member states, starting with the 1957 Treaty of Rome. Important changes were made through the Single European Act 1987, which established the single market, and the Treaty of Maastricht which came into force in 1993 and which included a timetable for economic and monetary union. These treaties created and developed the various legal instruments of the EU – such as directives and regulations – and the procedures for arriving at them.

The accumulated body of European community legislation is known by its French title, the *acquis communautaire*, to which any new member of the EU must subscribe. Directives have clear policy objectives and establish broad legal demands. Member states must then transpose directives into their own law, making sure that they give full effect to the purpose of the directive. If they fail to do so, or do so ineffectively, individuals can call on the EUROPEAN COURT OF JUSTICE (ECJ) for redress or guidance. In some cases individuals do not even have to wait on their national legislature. Where the ECJ considers an article of one of the treaties to be sufficiently clear and precise, individuals have recourse to the treaty itself. This has applied, for example, most notably in the use of Article 119 of the Treaty of Rome, which requires EQUAL PAY for equal work.

Important directives which directly impinge on employment include those covering:

- Equal pay and equal treatment
- HEALTH AND SAFETY
- Protection of pregnant women at work
- WORKING TIME
- Proof of an employment relationship
- TRANSFER OF UNDERTAKINGS
- Collective redundancies
- European works councils
- PARENTAL LEAVE
- Rights for workers on short-term assignments abroad

EWC
European works council (see WORKS COUNCIL).

EXIT INTERVIEW
The process of asking employees why they decide to leave their jobs. The main aim is to discover weaknesses in an organisation, such as why it has a high turnover of staff or finds it difficult to keep

talented staff. But the interview may also provide a defence against a subsequent claim for CONSTRUCTIVE DISMISSAL, or it may alert the company to a potential BREACH OF CONTRACT by the employee. This may be worthwhile in theory, but employees cannot be forced to attend an exit interview or to give their reasons for leaving if they do attend. Furthermore, the little research that has been done on exit interviews in the UK and the USA concluded that the majority of those interviewed did not reveal the true or full reason for their departure at their exit interview. For obvious reasons, an exit interview is likely to be more revealing if it is conducted by someone other than the employee's immediate boss.

> *It was astonishing. A new vice-president was sent in, gave my boss six days to get out, and fired me before we had exchanged ten words. I counted them.*
> Paul Hirsch, *Pack your own Parachute*

EXPENSES

Personal money, which the employer will refund, used by an employee to purchase essential goods or services while following company instructions. The most common expenses are the purchase of travel, food and accommodation. If the rules governing out-of-pocket expenses and the procedures for claiming them are not made clear, an employee may incur expenditure believing that it will be repaid only to discover it will not. It is the responsibility of managers to ensure that staff understand what will and what will not be reimbursed. General rules can be covered in the STAFF HANDBOOK, but anything specific to a particular job should be in the CONTRACT OF EMPLOYMENT or an individual letter.

EXTENDED LEAVE

When employees want to take more HOLIDAY than they are entitled to under their CONTRACT OF EMPLOYMENT, it is up to the employer to decide whether this will be allowed and on what terms. It is sensible for an employer to have a policy on extended leave so that decisions about it are seen to be fair. For example, it might be restricted to special circumstances, such as a once-in-a-lifetime visit to relatives overseas, or to certain periods during the year. It is usually unpaid. Some organisations allow a specified number of days of holiday to be carried over to the next year; others may give employees the option of a sabbatical as a break from a stressful job or at a certain stage in their career.

Where employees take more holiday than they are entitled to without their employer's permission they may face disciplinary action. If an employer specifies a date for the employee to return to work and it is ignored, the employer cannot regard the contract of employment as automatically terminated. The DISCIPLINARY PROCEDURE should always be followed; there may be some valid reason for the late return.

EYE TEST

From January 1st 1997 all new computer DISPLAY SCREEN EQUIPMENT must comply with EU controls covering radiation emissions from the screen and the quality and stability of the image. Free eye tests must be available every ten years for employees using the equipment. If an employee's eyesight has deteriorated as a result of screen work, the employer must help pay for corrective glasses.

FIDELITY

The simple concept that an employee must be loyal to an employer. It is implied in every CONTRACT OF EMPLOYMENT that employees will be honest, will not give away secrets to outsiders and will generally support the organisation. A business concerned with sensitive issues, relating, for example, to inventions, finance or stockmarkets, can put a fidelity clause in the contract that says what can or cannot be done. This will make it easier to dismiss or sue an employee if things go wrong.

FIGHTING

Behaviour that is unacceptable at work unless you are, say, a professional boxer. The CULTURE of the company and the country will determine when violence or threats of VIOLENCE become a disciplinary matter. Fighting can give grounds for instant (summary) DISMISSAL even, so the courts have said, if the disciplinary code does not directly state that it can. Usually, it is best to initiate a cooling-off period during which the incident can be investigated, not only in fairness to the parties involved but also because the reasons for the fight may demand further action; for example, to stop BULLYING or racial HARASSMENT. If no explanation can be found for the fight, employers are usually justified in disciplining all the parties involved.

FIXED-TERM CONTRACT

Contracts of employment that have a fixed duration have become widespread in recent years, particularly in continental Europe. They may be for a set period of time or relate to the completion of a specific role in, say, a research project or an IT installation. In essence, the contract will end on a set date or event.

Employers like fixed-term contracts because they appear to reduce overheads and make it easier to dispense with employees when they are not needed. But the LAW is beginning to give job security and other protection to workers on such contracts so their attractions are diminishing.

Here are some tips for employers wanting to use fixed-term contracts.

- Know why you are offering a fixed-term contract (rather than one of indefinite length).
- Check on current case law and legislative proposals.
- Recognise that the ending and non-renewal of a fixed-term contract equals DISMISSAL in law and may give grounds for a claim of REDUNDANCY or UNFAIR DISMISSAL.
- Do not assume you can change the conditions of employment without agreement when you offer work again.
- Try to avoid gaps of more than four weeks between periods of work or pay a retainer if you wish to avoid redundancy claims.

FLEXIBLE BENEFITS

The non-cash elements of an employee's reward package, such as PENSIONS, private medical insurance, COMPANY CARS. A flexible benefit system allows staff to choose which of the benefits on offer they want or whether they would prefer to receive the cash equivalent. When first implemented in the USA the system was frequently called "cafeteria benefits".

When a scheme is first set up staff will be told the total value available for benefits in their personal reward package. Knowing what each item is worth, they can then put together a personal portfolio of benefits. They may choose the minimum pension or an enhanced pension; private medical insurance for themselves only or for their whole family; a Mercedes or a Mini instead of a Mondeo, or even no car at all. Having made their choice they may have either underspent on their personal benefit value and will receive the balance in cash, or purchased extra benefits that must be paid for out of their salary.

Few schemes allow staff to forgo all the benefits offered in favour of cash. For example, most employers consider it to be irresponsible to allow people to opt out of the pension provision, although this rule may be relaxed if the other partner in a relationship has pension arrangements elsewhere.

The implementation of such schemes has been slow in both the USA and Europe. Research suggests that employers assume they are difficult to implement, costly to administer and "just a gimmick". Those that have implemented schemes say that none of this is true. Ask the staff of these employers what they think. The answer is always: "It's great to have a choice."

FLEXIBLE WORKFORCE

This has been a buzzword for employers and governments alike for several years. Organisations, it is argued, must be flexible, in terms of skills, employee deployment and labour use strategies. They should carefully analyse their need for functional flexibility, that is skills flexibility, and numerical flexibility, that is employing people on part-time, short-term contracts, for example, or OUTSOURCING to contractors or employment agencies for specialist or extra skills when they are needed.

The flexible employer is well established in the UK, the USA and increasingly in Europe, where there has been a huge growth in fixed-term and part-time employment. The flexible workforce – a core of staff with flexible skills and job security, supplemented by others employed as and when necessary – is also well established, especially in the public sector. There appear to be sound economic reasons for adopting the strategy. However, some key questions arise.

- How can you ask for commitment, loyalty and productivity from peripheral and essentially insecure staff?
- How can you ensure your training needs are met and can develop in a flexible workforce?
- Does the flexible core carry an excess burden in terms of work demands, working

hours and generally keeping the show on the road?
- What are the real costs of constant recruitment, re-recruitment and TRANSACTIONAL MANAGEMENT of the periphery?
- How much time is spent on recruiting, inducting, training and documenting the contracts of short-term employees?
- How do you ensure quality of product and service delivery with a flexible workforce?

It is essential that flexible policies are assessed regularly to ensure their real, as opposed to imagined, effectiveness.

So long as flexible means efficient, rather than cheap, everyone will benefit. If flexible working is misused and is an excuse to avoid responsibility for holidays, maternity pay and leaving notice... employers will be rewarded with a lack of commitment.
Alex Reed, Reed Personal Services, 1995

FOCUS GROUP
A group of employees brought together to review and comment on a specific aspect of company work. They are often used to enhance an organisation's understanding of problems highlighted by an EMPLOYEE OPINION SURVEY. In this case the focus group is usually chaired by an external agency, which presents a confidential report to top management expanding on the comments but protecting the identities of the commentators.

FREEDOM OF MOVEMENT
The 1957 Treaty of Rome, which established the European Economic Community (EEC), guaranteed the right of free movement of workers belonging to the member states within the EEC and provided for their right to stay in any member state for the purpose of employment. As a result, EU nationals do not need work permits to take up employment in any member state, although they may need res-

idence permits. However, many practical and legal barriers to free movement remain; in particular, language differences, differing social security arrangements, and varying educational and vocational training systems. The European Union has sought to provide for the mutual recognition of a number of professional QUALIFICATIONS, although the practical implementation for individual professions has often been complex and protracted. In addition, guidelines of equivalence have been developed for other vocational qualifications.

FREELANCE STAFF

A term used typically in the media and related occupations to refer to people working on a SELF-EMPLOYED basis. Employers should check that such people are genuinely self-employed (see EMPLOYMENT STATUS).

FRUSTRATION

Business is often frustrating, but this is a situation in LAW whereby events outside your control (such as war and natural disasters) make it impossible for a contract to begin or continue. If a contract is frustrated no one is to blame and neither party can sue the other. On rare occasions chronic ILLNESS, imprisonment or, say, the kidnapping of an employee entitle an employer to argue that a contract of employment has become impossible and is therefore at an end. But such problems are usually better handled through an organisation's normal human resources procedures.

GANTT CHART

A task represented by a straight line proportional to the time allowed to achieve it, with a second line drawn above to show the achievement. This may seem obvious to us, but it was unheard of before Henry Gantt invented it at the end of the 19th century. He worked with F.W. Taylor at the Bethlehem Steel Works, and helped to implement SCIENTIFIC MANAGEMENT.

GARDEN LEAVE

Employees who have access to financial or market-sensitive information that could be of use to a rival organisation may have a garden leave clause in their CONTRACT OF EMPLOYMENT. If they resign, this allows their employer to require them to spend their NOTICE period (providing it is not unreasonably long and that they are paid) tending their garden or doing something equally innocuous, thus denying them further access to any commercially valuable information. The term is also used sometimes to refer to employees who have been suspended.

GENUINE OCCUPATIONAL QUALIFICATION

The Sex Discrimination Act 1975 and the Race Relations Act 1976 provide that the restrictions on DISCRIMINATION do not apply where being of a particular sex or racial group is a genuine occupational qualification for the job. Examples given are dramatic performances, such as playing Othello, the preservation of decency or privacy, such as a lavatory attendant, and duties in countries with different customs or laws.

GIFT

Many organisations have policies on employees receiving gifts. Usually gifts of a nominal value, such as a bottle of wine, are acceptable, but those of a more substantial nature are not. In the UK a gift is treated as a benefit in kind and is therefore taxable (see TIP).

GRIEVANCE PROCEDURE

The way an organisation deals with grievances brought to its attention by employees. The aim of a formal procedure is to provide a system for grievances to be aired and dealt with in a non-confrontational way, thus avoiding the risk of simmering dissent boiling over and creating a serious problem. In UK LAW most employers are required to provide information on their formal grievance procedure by the Employment Rights Act 1996. Here are some useful guidelines.

- The person to whom grievances should first be notified must be someone an employee can trust. It should not be their immediate superior since a large number of grievances at work concern employees' immediate bosses.
- Time limits should be set for each stage of the procedure to provide certainty and comfort to both employee and employer. The employee knows that the complaint cannot be ignored, and the company knows that it cannot be dragged out by the employee.

It is important that all employees are aware of their organisation's grievance procedure. Many companies publish the details in a STAFF HANDBOOK, often linking the grievance procedure with the DISCIPLINARY PROCEDURE so that appeals against disciplinary decisions can be treated as grievances, thus avoiding the need for a separate disciplinary appeals procedure.

GURU

A Hindi word meaning "spiritual teacher", which has been adopted to label the more profound thinkers and writers in the field of management style, management techniques, organisational change, LEADERSHIP, and how best to manage and motivate people.

HANDLING LOADS

More people suffer back injury as a result of work than any other injury. It costs employers and national economies huge sums of money each year in lost work, SICK PAY and COMPENSATION. European legislation, enacted in the UK in the Manual Handling Regulations 1992, requires employers to assess the risks caused by lifting loads. If these are significant they must consider their options, for example, using automatic lifting equipment, changing the weight or size of loads and improving training. In the UK the Health and Safety Executive and other national agencies provide a lot of advice and information. Failure to comply with the law can lead to heavy fines and/or compensation to victims.

HARASSMENT

Persistent offensive behaviour towards an employee, which is of a racial or sexual nature. The essential definition of sexual harassment is that it is not wanted by the recipient. In practice it can range from unwelcome physical contact, innuendo and even blatantly displayed "girlie" calendars. Racial harassment may take many forms, including racist jokes and banter, name calling, practical jokes, unwelcome gifts, displays of racist publications, physical assault. It is important for employers to make harassment a disciplinary offence because in certain circumstances they can be held equally liable under the Sex Discrimination Act 1975 or the Race Relations Act 1976 for harassment committed by an employee, even if they had no knowledge of it. Similarly, an employer's failure to treat a complaint of harassment seriously, or to deal with it adequately, may give rise to a complaint of RACIAL or SEXUAL DISCRIMINATION. (See also DIGNITY AT WORK.)

Sexual harassment is the subject of specific legislation in a number of EU countries, including France and Germany. In most cases the laws build on the employer's DUTY OF CARE and existing criminal LAW on assault, often adding a precise definition of the offence.

HAWTHORNE EXPERIMENTS

Between 1927 and 1932 Western Electric conducted research into working conditions at the Hawthorne Works in Chicago. Two teams of female workers were used; one was the control and the other was subjected to many different working conditions. An Australian industrial sociologist, Elton Mayo, led the research, changing the hours worked and shift patterns, varying rest breaks and the lighting intensity, repainting the factory walls, offering new incentives and shorter hours, and so on. Each time a change was made output increased. Absenteeism decreased by 80%, and even the control team increased its output, although not as much as the change team. Then the change team were asked to return to their original working conditions – a 48-hour week, no rest breaks, no incentives – and output rose again to the highest level ever recorded at Hawthorne.

Mayo concluded that the interest taken in the groups by the company, and the fact that people were constantly communicating with the workers (the researchers always discussed the work and explained the research), led them to feel more valued and more responsible for their performance. This sense of TEAM cohesion and self-esteem was deemed more important to performance than any change in working conditions. The research revealed the importance of human emotions and respect for others in the workplace.

HEADHUNTER

Jargon for a specialist consultant, more formally referred to as an executive search consultant, employed by a client to recruit key staff. For companies, the advantages of using search consultants are that they should be knowledgeable about the market and able to advise on the REMUNERATION package that will be needed to attract the right type of person. They should also already know some potential candidates and be able to identify others reasonably quickly. Following an initial discussion, interested candidates can be interviewed to produce a shortlist to recommend to the client.

As well as the skills they bring to the job, headhunters, if they take the trouble to properly understand their clients and their needs, can save companies time and money on RECRUITMENT. Despite its perceived high cost, the process is usually less costly and time-consuming than advertising, screening and interviewing, and it is more likely to produce a better result. Some take the view that it is unethical to approach people already in jobs. Although many EU countries have severely circumscribed the activities of private employment agencies in the past, if less so now, for the most part executive search has been permitted or tolerated. However, headhunters must be careful to describe themselves as advising on appointments and not suggest that they are engaged in placement activity. The largest executive search markets outside the UK are in Germany and France.

People so often see health and safety awareness as a sign of weakness.
Sir Bob Reid, when chairman of British Rail, 1993

HEALTH AND SAFETY

Regulations governing health and safety at work are sometimes accused of being a burden on business, nit-picking and tiresome. Yet poor health and safety standards can cost employers a lot in terms of accidents, ill-health, loss of productivity, high INSURANCE premiums, disruption and adverse publicity, especially when there is a major accident involving many deaths and injuries, such as the Piper Alpha North Sea oil rig fire or the leak of poisonous fumes from a chemical plant in Seveso, in northern Italy.

Poorly maintained PREMISES, dangerous equipment, or a workplace that is too hot, too dusty, too noisy or too prone to violence, will have an adverse effect on employee health, business efficiency and costs. Most countries recognise that self-regulation by employers will not ensure adequate safety standards across the board, so a great many laws setting minimum health and safety standards have been enacted throughout the developed world. In Europe a lot of work has been done to identify workplace hazards and those most at risk from them with a view to framing legislation in a way that will effectively minimise the risks. Regardless of the issue – machinery, buildings, DISPLAY SCREEN EQUIPMENT, noise, hazardous chemicals or other substances – EUROPEAN LAW has a basic and consistent approach. Employers must:

- assess all risks at the workplace to employees and others;
- take appropriate steps to minimise risks, for example, by introducing better maintenance, new machinery, and better training and supervision of staff;
- regularly monitor, review and, if necessary, improve health and safety standards.

The key to good standards is good management. Employers should:

- provide adequate resources for health and safety;
- fully support health and safety standards;
- take specialist advice on developing and instituting health and safety policies;
- ensure all managers are aware of their health and safety responsibilities;
- make sure that health and safety issues are included in all organisational decision-making and activities.

The problem for employers today is that they are increasingly responsible for the safety standards not only of their own employees but also of those over whom they have less control, such as contractors, AGENCY STAFF and the SELF-EMPLOYED.

HEALTH CHECK
See MEDICAL EXAMINATION.

HEALTH RECORD

A record covering the physical or mental health of an employee. In the UK the Access to Health Records Act 1990 applies to records held by the health professional who created them or for whom they were created. Health professionals include registered medical practitioners, registered nurses, midwives or health visitors, clinical psychologists, registered dentists, registered opticians, registered chiropodists, occupational therapists, orthopaedists and physiotherapists. Employees have a legal right to see their own health records. Access can be denied when, in the opinion of the holder of the record, providing the information would be likely to cause serious physical or mental harm to the individual or would reveal the identity of a third party (without that party's consent) who has given information about the employee concerned. It is also denied where the information was gathered before the Health Records Act came into force, unless it is needed to clarify another part of the record to which the individual does have access. Employers or prospective employers can see the records only if authorised by the employee or prospective employee. If an employee thinks the record is incorrect, misleading or incomplete, he or she can apply for corrections to be made giving the reasons or evidence for the inaccuracy.

HIERARCHY OF NEEDS

Created by Abraham Maslow in the late 1940s to account for the roots of human motivation. The theory postulates that once the individual's basic physiological needs are satisfied, the next higher need becomes the motivator. Maslow's pyramid of needs is as follows.

Level 1 Physiological: the need for food, water, shelter and sex.
Level 2 Safety and security: the need for protection against danger and the loss of the Level 1 physiological needs; a desire for stability, order and predictability.

Level 3 Social: the need for love, affection, acceptance and belonging to a group.

Level 4 (a) Self-esteem: the need to have a stable, firmly based, high evaluation of self; the desire for achievement, adequacy, confidence in the face of the world, independence and freedom.

(b) Respect: the need to have the respect of others, manifested by recognition, attention, importance or appreciation.

Level 5 Self-fulfilment: the need to develop to our full potential, to be creative, to feel we are contributing something worthwhile; to become what we believe we are capable of becoming.

More recent researchers have decided that Maslow's hierarchy is too simplistic and there is much more to human motivation. However, his work remains the basis of much current thinking.

HOLIDAY

Everyone needs a break from work. The average holiday entitlement for employees varies from country to country; for example, in the USA it is two weeks, in the UK it is four weeks and in Germany workers enjoy an average of some six weeks. In the UK until recently there was no legal requirement for employers to give employees holidays, either paid or unpaid. The EU Working Time Directive 1993, implemented in November 1996, provides for three weeks' paid holiday for all. Most employers go beyond this, and paid holiday is the norm. As with other issues, the important elements should be clearly understood by the employee; for example, how much holiday, whether it is paid, when it can be taken, the dates of the holiday year, how many days' holiday (if any) can be carried over to the next holiday year and who approves holiday requests.

HOMEWORKING

Getting people to do their work at home has been one method employers have used to cut their overheads in recent years. Homeworkers now fall into two distinct groups: traditional homeworkers, such as those who make items of clothing; and teleworkers, that is those who carry out computer-based work. Recent research indicates that the forecast growth in homeworking has not occurred. Homeworking involves less than 1% of the workforce in the vast majority of organisations in European countries. The reasons for this lack of growth include technology costs, managers being reluctant to lose contact with (and control over) their staff and problems with co-ordination. For the individuals involved, the disadvantage of homeworking is that they may feel isolated and alienated from the company they are working for. A European Commission research study found that over 25% of home-based teleworkers suffered from STRESS, compared with less than 10% of the general population. Employers can help reduce the sense of isolation by including homeworkers in office-based activities from time to time.

Homeworkers may be employees or they may be SELF-EMPLOYED. The courts use a variety of tests to determine people's EMPLOYMENT STATUS, including mutuality of obligation. UK tribunals and courts generally find homeworkers to be employees. A homeworker in the UK, who is an employee of a company and is employed for one month or more, is entitled to receive a written STATEMENT OF TERMS OF WORK within two months of starting the job. The terms and conditions in the contract should clarify the working arrangements. Subjects that may be covered are:

- equipment – installation costs;
- use and security of equipment;
- HEALTH AND SAFETY requirements;
- working times;
- ABSENCE – not available for work, sickness;
- basis of payment.

The terms and conditions should also be comparable with those for office-based employees.

The Health and Safety at Work Act 1974 and the Management of Health and Safety at Work Regulations 1992 give some protection to homeworkers and other people in the household in respect of hazards arising from work taken into the home. If computers are used the Health and Safety (Display Screen Equipment) Regulations 1992 must be complied with. Rest periods, work routines, eye tests and HOURS OF WORK are just some of the issues that should be considered.

It is important for employers to ensure homeworkers have the appropriate skills and are performing in line with requirements. They should also provide training if necessary and operate an APPRAISAL system. Depending on the nature of the job, career development opportunities may exist. If a homeworker's personal circumstances change, a move to the organisation's PREMISES to work either full-time or part-time may be in the company's and the employee's interests.

HOURS OF WORK

The number of hours of work a week that employers offer employees is a matter of choice, although the details must be included in their STATEMENT OF TERMS OF WORK. Similarly, hours can be flexible and extended hours can be paid or unpaid. New regulations as a result of EUROPEAN LAW will require breaks from work on a daily, weekly and annual basis (paid HOLIDAY) and limit NIGHT WORK. This is sensible, as long, unbroken hours of work are a major cause of STRESS and other ILLNESS. All European countries apart from the UK have restrictions on working hours. The key provisions of the EU Working Time Directive 1993 (operative since 1996) are that workers should have:

- a continuous period of 11 hours' break in 24 hours;
- a continuous break period of 35 hours per week;
- a normal week of less than 48 hours, unless the employee has agreed to work longer;
- a night shift of usually no more than 8 hours;
- 3 (4 eventually) weeks' paid holiday per year.

Many industries and occupations, such as transport, hospitals and residential care, have some flexibility. UK legislation is awaited to implement the directive.

> *Motivation comes from within the individual; it is not created by the organisation according to some formula.*
> Frederick Herzberg

HYGIENE FACTORS

Frederick Herzberg's research into motivation revealed that what satisfied and dissatisfied employees arose from quite different factors. It had been assumed that dissatisfaction was simply an opposing reaction to the same factors that satisfied. Herzberg called the satisfiers motivational factors and the dissatisfiers hygiene factors.

The motivators were:

- a sense of achievement;
- recognition;
- responsibility;
- progress;
- personal growth.

The hygiene factors were:

- SALARY;
- job security;
- status;
- interpersonal relations;
- company policy and procedures;
- working conditions.

Herzberg concluded that we must minimise the dissatisfaction caused by poor hygiene factors, many of which clearly relate to the bottom levels of Abraham Maslow's HIERARCHY OF NEEDS, and then focus management effort on the motivating factors, which represent the top level of Maslow's hierarchy. Herzberg's theories have helped breed such developments as JOB ENRICHMENT, flexitime and FLEXIBLE BENEFITS.

ILLEGAL EMPLOYMENT CONTRACT

This sounds exciting and it is, but such contracts cannot be enforced. If you make a deal that, say, someone will be treated (unlawfully) as a limited company, or will act as a drugs courier or contract killer, this is an illegal contract. If the deal goes wrong neither side can sue (nor can an employee claim UNFAIR DISMISSAL). Where the employee is genuinely innocent, because, for example, he did not know he was transporting illegal drugs or immigrants, a court should give him some rights, but it is always tricky for those who find themselves working for a crook.

INCAPACITY BENEFIT

A benefit available in the UK for those who cannot work because of ILLNESS or DISABILITY. It is not available if an employee is receiving statutory SICK PAY from an employer, or if an individual is over the state retirement age. The benefit is not dependent on other earnings and is not taxed for the first 28 weeks. It is not an automatic benefit and must be applied for.

INCOMES POLICY

Although incomes policies have become highly unfashionable in the UK, tripartite (union–employer–government) control over pay increases has by no means died out elsewhere in Europe. Ireland, for example, has had a successful voluntary incomes policy since 1987, with high compliance by business. Incomes policies have also been agreed, or imposed, in the Netherlands and in Belgium, where pay increases can be tied to those of Belgium's main international competitors if the economy is losing its edge.

INDUSTRIAL ACTION

Action taken by employees in furtherance of a dispute with their employer may take the form of a strike, a go-slow, an overtime ban, picketing or working to rule. There is no such thing as a right to strike in UK LAW. If employees go on strike or take other industrial action it is a serious BREACH OF

CONTRACT. This means the employer can dismiss the employees without NOTICE.

Secondary action occurs when, for example, TRADE UNION members picket the site of a company at which the members are not employees. Trade unions in the UK have no legal immunity in civil law in respect of such action. Secondary action directed at associated companies within a group is also unlawful, as long as employees in the associated company have separate contracts of employment.

The legal position varies considerably in other European countries. In most cases the law (more typically the constitution) grants a positive right to strike, with employees suspending but not breaching their contracts of employment by withdrawing their labour. The extent to which this right is qualified by other legislation or court rulings varies considerably. In Germany, for example, the 1948 Basic Law (the constitution) merely grants employers and employees the right to form associations to pursue their economic interests. All regulations on what is and what is not lawful have been developed by the courts, with fairly strict limits on spontaneous action and a ban on strikes during the lifetime of an agreement. In contrast, French law views the right to strike as an individual right. Strikes are not subject to much legal regulation and, in the absence of strong unions offering organisation and strike pay, strikes in France have a propensity to be sudden, short, sometimes violent and characterised by innovative tactics.

The UK Trade Union and Labour Relations (Consolidation) Act 1992 defines strikes as "any concerted stoppage of work". The rights of workers to withdraw their labour without fear of criminal or other types of proceedings is well established. This immunity is provided as long as the strike falls within the conditions laid out in the act. The UK's strike record is now among the lowest in Europe, along with Germany and the Netherlands. In 1994, for example, 13 days were lost per 1,000 workers through strikes in the UK compared with 8 in the Netherlands, 9 in Germany, 26 in France, 246 in Italy and 329 in Greece.

Normally strikers will not receive any REMUNERATION from their employer during the strike. The action of striking does not automatically end an employee's CONTRACT OF EMPLOYMENT, but an employer may dismiss those who strike and an individual cannot then claim UNFAIR DISMISSAL if the employer:

- has dismissed everyone taking part in the strike at the same establishment at the same time;
- has offered re-engagement to all of them within three months of their date of dismissal.

Strikes are called for various reasons, but the most common is to obtain increases in PAY and improvements in conditions of service. The most effective way of avoiding strikes is through continual open communication and CONSULTATION with the workforce. The more the employees understand how a company is performing and why activities are planned and implemented, the less likely they are to go on strike.

INDUSTRIAL ENGINEERING
Techniques aimed specifically at improving productivity. They cover improvement in four main areas.

- Conditions: ERGONOMICS
- Organisations: operational research
- Methods and procedures: TIME AND MOTION STUDY, planning, LABOUR COSTS
- Products and services: value analysis, total quality management

INDUSTRIAL ESPIONAGE
Every business likes to know what its competitors are up to regarding new inventions, marketing strategies, takeovers, and so on, and some will resort to covert means to find out. Industrial espionage can involve criminal acts such as breaking

and entering or stealing, or civil wrongs such as a BREACH OF CONTRACT of employment or of a confidentiality agreement. Any employee involved in passing on important secret information about their employer can normally be instantly dismissed and sued for damages. If a CRIMINAL ACT is involved the police can be brought in.

> *Organisations always lag behind strategy. Because of the assumption that you have to know what it is you want to do before you can know how to do it, all organisations based on the industrial model are created for businesses that either no longer exist or are in the process of going out of existence.*
> Stanley M. Davis

INDUSTRIAL TRIBUNAL

Established in 1964 to deal with minor bureaucratic issues, industrial tribunals now handle thousands of disputes involving REDUNDANCY, UNFAIR DISMISSAL, unlawful DEDUCTIONS FROM PAY, DISCRIMINATION and BREACH OF CONTRACT. Around 60% of claims are withdrawn or settled outside the tribunal. The success rate of the rest is variable and employers do not inevitably lose. The level of COMPENSATION is still fairly low, despite occasional press reports that give the impression that a successful claimant has hit the jackpot.

Anyone wanting to make a claim against a current or former employer must fill in a form (IT1) outlining the complaint. Officials check that the claim has potential and the claimant is qualified (for example, has any necessary CONTINUITY of service) before passing the form to the employer, now called the respondent, who fills in form IT2 outlining any defence. The forms are then passed to ACAS, which will try to obtain an agreed settlement.

Industrial tribunal claims can be time consuming and cause problems even before they come to a full hearing. Claims can be rejected as vexatious and frivolous, but few are. There is usually a pre-hearing review, conducted by a chairman, which assesses the likelihood of a win by either the claimant or the employer. If it is an open and shut case it should not go to a full hearing. An increasing number of cases are heard by an industrial tribunal chairman alone, without the usual "wing persons" who have experience of the world of work. The aim of this is to speed things up, and there are plans to improve the ways of filtering out weak claims. A full hearing can last from a few hours to several days and, although more informal (no wigs and less rigorous rules of evidence, for example) than a law court, hearings are highly structured. It is not essential to have legal representation; the chairman has a duty to assist litigants who are not legally represented in the presentation of their cases. However, a lawyer will improve the chance of success.

The experience of industrial tribunals suggests the following.

- There is no substitute for good personnel procedures which have been carefully and fairly followed. The strongest defence of a claim can be ruined by misuse of procedures. Even when outraged by an employee's behaviour, an employer should keep calm, follow procedures, and do so with TRANSPARENCY.
- A successful outcome depends as much on careful preparation for a hearing as well as good grounds. All the relevant witnesses should attend the hearing because evidence must come from the people concerned.
- Allow time for the hearing and expect delays and disruption. Hearings rarely run smoothly.
- Do not patronise the tribunal or make assumptions; for example, that the officials have knowledge of the workplace, its CULTURE and its priorities.
- Be prepared for the other party to be aggressive or emotional.
- Be sensitive to the dilemma of other employees or ex-employees called to give

evidence; few people are willing or enthusiastic witnesses.
- Do not count on others, especially the "wing-persons", sharing your view of the world of work.
- Co-operate fully with the tribunal officials and ACAS; both groups are highly professional and impartial.

INJUNCTION

A useful legal device that can be used to prevent imminent or continuing harm to an organisation in the case of, say, an unlawful strike or an employee giving valuable data to a rival. Injunctions are easily and cheaply obtained from a judge, who will often grant an interim injunction if a *prima facie* case can be shown; that is, there are reasonable grounds for considering harm may be caused. This does not mean, however, that the injunction will not be lifted at the full court hearing. Failure to comply with an injunction can lead to imprisonment. Injunctions can also be obtained against employers, for example, where they threaten to dismiss staff contrary to contractual procedures.

INJURY AT WORK

See ACCIDENTS AT WORK; DAMAGES; HANDLING LOADS; HEALTH AND SAFETY; NEGLIGENCE.

INSOLVENCY

The inability of an organisation to pay its debts as and when they become due. Insolvency may lead to a receiver being appointed to try and sort things out and it may result in the business going into liquidation. During receivership employees' contracts continue, but any employees leaving the sinking ship will be deemed to have resigned rather than to have been dismissed for REDUNDANCY purposes. There are complex rules about the liability for WAGES and other payments during receivership. If the organisation goes into liquidation, employees are redundant and can claim against their ex-employer. If there are no funds to pay them, the Department of Trade and Industry picks up the tab under the Employment Rights Act 1996. If the ailing organisation is bought by someone else, the employees are transferred according to the usual rules (see TRANSFER OF UNDERTAKINGS).

INSURANCE

Many of an organisation's activities can be covered by insurance in case things go wrong. There might be an accident, fire or THEFT that might involve third parties as well as employees and SELF-EMPLOYED people. It is also possible (and wise) to insure against the costs of maternity leave, REDUNDANCY and employment statutory claims.

It is important to note that the burden of statutory employment rights, including SICK PAY, is gradually moving to the employer, especially in the UK. However, the mechanisms for the provision of insurance cover vary from country to country. In some, such as Spain, private insurance companies provide the cover; in some, such as Germany, the state controls most of the arrangements; and in others, such as the UK, there is a mixture of state and private provision.

The costs of accidents and the consequent payouts by insurers have grown enormously. There is a general move away from flat-rate contributions to contributions based on the standards and claim records of organisations. This system has considerable merit, ensuring that "good" employers are not subsidising "bad" ones.

INTELLECTUAL PROPERTY

The creative element of a product, such as the software program rather than the disk containing it and the design of a car rather than the car itself. Businesses normally want employees to be inventive and creative. Where the business is involved in high technology, fashion, entertainment, education, and so on, inventiveness may be the most important element of the job. But when a new product, design or process is developed, who owns the rights and can claim royalties paid in respect of those rights on sales of the finished product or on licensing the design?

The rule is that, in principle, if the creative work took place in the course of employment the rights belong to the employer. Where the situation is unclear the creator can claim under the Patent Act 1977 for a fair share of the royalties. The wise course for an organisation is to make plain in a policy document or the CONTRACT OF EMPLOYMENT what the position is, especially with regard to grey areas where the creative work is only a part of the employee's job.

INTERVIEW
See DISCIPLINARY PROCEDURE; RECRUITMENT.

INVENTION
See INTELLECTUAL PROPERTY.

Any business which evaluates effectively will know the return on its investment in people. It will know that it is getting results. It is making the most of its money. It is doing the things it needs to do to survive and grow. It is delivering what its customers want. It is getting the most from its people.
Investors in People

INVESTORS IN PEOPLE
A UK government sponsored initiative through which companies are publicly recognised as having taken action "to improve the skills, knowledge, motivation, commitment, confidence and job satisfaction of all its people". The benefits of the initiative are that it encourages companies to think about, and create a policy and strategy for, the training and development of their staff. The drawbacks, articulated by many, are that it is bureaucratic, paper intensive and assessed by procedure-bound third-rate consultants from the TRAINING AND ENTERPRISE COUNCILS.

ITEMISED PAY STATEMENT
Under the UK Employment Rights Act 1996, all employees, other than certain excluded categories

such as police officers, have the right at or before pay-day to receive from their employer a written itemised pay statement. This must contain the following details.

- The gross amount of WAGES or SALARY.
- The amounts of and reasons for any variable or fixed deductions from the gross payment, for example, TRADE UNION subscriptions.
- The net amount of wages or salary payable.
- The amount and method of each payment if different parts of the net amount are paid in different ways.

JOBCENTRE

The 1,079 Jobcentres in the UK were designed to be more up-to-date, useful and welcoming places than the labour exchange offices they replaced. Now they are perhaps the most undervalued and under-utilised of the government's employment support services.

For employers they provide the following services.

- A national computer database of vacancies.
- Advice on RECRUITMENT methods and procedures.
- Information about the local labour market.
- Information on the availability of suitable candidates.
- Distribution of an employer's job application forms.
- Free interviewing rooms.
- Assessment and pre-selection of candidates against an employer's criteria.
- Work trial periods at no cost to the employer.

For those looking for work they provide the following programmes and services.

- **Job Search Plus:** a three-day course to help define goals, identify potential employers, write a CV and prepare for interviews, plus a fortnightly review of progress.
- **Job Interview Guarantee:** offers a full assessment of potential and guarantees an interview with a prospective employer.
- **Job Preparation Course:** provides a full understanding of the job and helps prepare for the interview.
- **Travel to Interview Scheme:** helps with the cost of travelling to an interview.
- **Back to Work Incentive Scheme:** employers who take on someone who has been unemployed for two years or more do not have to pay the employer's NATIONAL INSURANCE contribution for that employee for

the first 12 months.
- **Access to Work Programme:** helps disabled people to get jobs. As well as special recruitment assistance, employers can get government help to make a workplace accessible and working conditions suitable for a person with a DISABILITY.

JOB DESCRIPTION

Every job has certain aims and involves certain tasks and responsibilities that can be outlined in a job description. Such documents can be used to:

- help structure the roles of employees in a department or work unit, ensuring both the manager and the employee have a common understanding of what is required;
- assist in identifying the training and development needs of an individual;
- assist in the RECRUITMENT and selection process;
- evaluate jobs.

Unfortunately, job descriptions often sit in filing cabinets for years, gathering dust when they should be referred to at regular intervals – for example, at a performance APPRAISAL interview – and kept up to date in order to reflect how a job has changed.

Job descriptions come in a variety of forms, but it is common to have a section entitled "principle purpose" outlining in one or two short paragraphs the reason the job exists. The next section usually details the main duties or responsibilities of the job. Other sections may include resources managed by the job or the competencies, qualifications and experience required. A manager or a job holder can draft the job description. Job holders may be given the task to encourage them to think about how their job can be developed. The way the job description is written is partly prescribed by the use that will be made of it. (See also ROLE DESCRIPTION.)

JOB ENRICHMENT

A method of enhancing work by motivational factors (mostly non-PAY) to meet the aspirations of employees. The term was coined by Frederick Herzberg, and was fashionable in the 1970s when companies were reviewing pay and working conditions in the light of Herzberg's HYGIENE FACTORS.

JOB EVALUATION

A process designed to measure the demands of the job, not the job holder's performance. Effective job evaluation schemes need to have the support of management and, if appropriate, trade unions and employees. It is not unusual to have joint management and TRADE UNION job evaluation panels; union support is essential if the results are to be used as the basis of COLLECTIVE BARGAINING.

Job evaluation is used to rank jobs in an order of worth within an organisation. Once grades have been established, SALARY scales can be developed and linked to them. As the process compares jobs rather than people, it can help in avoiding EQUAL PAY disputes.

The ways of evaluating jobs can be divided into three groups.

- Non-analytical schemes evaluate the whole job.
- Analytical points rating schemes analyse the job against predefined factors such as responsibility and then classify it by level of complexity.
- Competency-based schemes identify the competencies required to do a job and use this as the basis of the evaluation.

JOB SHARING

Two people who want to do PART-TIME WORK may be able to share a job; for example, one may work in the morning and the other in the afternoon, or each person may work for two and a half days. Employees who job share should be treated in the same way as other employees, and training, development and promotion opportunities should be equivalent.

There are advantages and disadvantages for an employer who introduces job sharing, so the management and administration of such a scheme must be carefully thought through in advance. Some of the advantages are:

- it is attractive to employees compared with ordinary PART-TIME WORK;
- it provides a wide range of skills and experience in one post;
- it provides cover for at least part of the job while one sharer is ill or on leave;
- there is generally a high level of productivity;
- it is a good indicator of a commitment to EQUAL OPPORTUNITY.

Some of the disadvantages are:

- the need to invest in management and communication systems;
- it can be disruptive, especially to outsiders who might not know what is going on;
- sharers can be somewhat inflexible.

In Europe job sharing is most common in the UK, although in Norway and Sweden it is beginning to be seen as a means of opening professional and managerial jobs to part-time workers.

What's good about job sharing? Well, two heads are better than one.
Senior civil servant, HM Treasury, 1992

JOB TITLE

Titles given to jobs should reflect, first, what the job is and second, if at all, its status. Inevitably, it is the latter that obsesses many. But as an indication of status a job title can be important for those who are dealing with outsiders. Some organisations give their sales staff two job titles, one for internal use and one for external use, because many clients want to deal with a "manager" or an "executive". DIRECTOR is also widely used in the job titles of people who do not have a seat on the board.

An organisation's hierarchy can be defined by the job titles used, for example, assistant manager, manager, general manager. The name of the function may also be added, for example, manager finance. Consideration should be given to internal comparisons of job titles before new job titles are created to ensure that there are no anomalies. For example, two management jobs of the same type in the same or a different function should have similar titles, such as assistant manager finance and assistant manager sales.

JOBSEEKER'S ALLOWANCE

The UK state unemployment benefit payable to those over 18 and below pensionable age, who are out of work, capable of work, and actively seeking employment.

JURY SERVICE

Everyone aged over 18 on the electoral roll, apart from members of a few groups such as lawyers and the armed forces, is liable for jury service. Although most organisations like to be thought of as being community minded, there is no law that says employers must continue to pay employees while they are serving on a jury. Jurors can claim a loss of earnings allowance and travelling expenses from the court. An employer dismissing a person on jury service for ABSENCE is liable for UNFAIR DISMISSAL, unless the employee had not given advance warning.

Anyone seeking to be excused when called for jury service must write to the court in question giving reasons for the request. The only reasons the court is likely to accept are that you are ill, deaf, blind, have a holiday already booked, or have a close connection to any party in the case.

Kaizen

A Japanese word meaning continuous improvement. W. Edwards Deming, who went to Japan in 1950 and became a production GURU there, based his philosophy on the premise that the customer is the most important part of the production line. Merely having a satisfied customer was not enough: "Profit in business comes from repeat customers, customers that boast about your products and services to their friends, so that they buy them." To achieve this, Deming said companies must "reduce variation". From this flowed QUALITY MANAGEMENT and continuous improvement.

Knowledge workers

People who deal with ever-changing information so complex that only they can understand it. Thus they cannot be told what to do, they cannot be directed, and they are difficult to manage in the traditional sense. They must be led, shown the VISION and the goal, and motivated to use their knowledge as only they know how. Management by dominance and fear are inappropriate, since the knowledge workers will rapidly vote with their feet. They see themselves as professionals to be treated with respect.

LABOUR COSTS

The costs of employing people. Productivity and competitiveness can depend on relative labour costs, especially in labour-intensive occupations such as catering, banking, leisure and healthcare. Labour costs are made up of WAGES or SALARY costs and non-wage costs such as social security, PENSIONS and other BENEFITS. These vary considerably from country to country with some, such as Sweden and Germany, having high non-wage costs. The extent of the differences is debatable. However, a true analysis of labour costs should include the following:

- Illness and ABSENCE costs
- Recruitment costs
- Induction
- Training
- TRANSACTIONAL MANAGEMENT costs

For some organisations these non-wage costs can be substantial, and they should certainly be taken into account when considering the advantages of flexible labour practices.

LANGUAGE OF EMPLOYMENT PRACTICE

In the global marketplace it is still important to remember that there are subtle and not-so-subtle differences between how the same thing is described. The LAW applying to employment relations is, for example, labour law in the USA, employment law in the UK and social law in the European Union (although individual member states also use labour law in courts, and so on). Similarly, in the EU employers and unions are referred to as SOCIAL PARTNERS, while those who find it hard to get jobs or benefits are "socially excluded". In the UK if there is no work to do you are "redundant"; in most EU countries you are dismissed for "economic reasons". The list could go on. It is, however, important to be aware not only of the terminological differences, but also the different approaches to employment relations that the language may indicate.

LATENESS

A form of absenteeism that an organisation's rules may define as MISCONDUCT. Lateness applies not only to the start of the working day, but also to the return from meal and other breaks and meetings and appointments within or outside the organisation. It is good practice to bring such lateness to the attention of any individuals concerned; they need to understand that it is not acceptable behaviour before you get to the DISCIPLINARY PROCEDURE stage.

An employer initiating disciplinary action because of an employee's lateness should ensure that the position has been monitored and there is a record giving times and dates, and that the employee cannot claim DISCRIMINATION on the ground that many others are equally at fault. (See also ABSENCE.)

LATERAL THINKING

Devised by Dr Edward de Bono in 1967, lateral thinking seeks to solve problems by unorthodox or apparently illogical methods. De Bono believes that most managers are trained to maintain things efficiently and to solve problems. A different set of thinking skills is required when seeking new business opportunities. (See also PARALLEL THINKING.)

> *When you return to your car on an icy day and the lock is frozen the vertical thinker may try to heat the lock with his lighter in the wind. The lateral thinker may shelter and heat his key with the flame.*
> Edward de Bono

LAW

It has been popular in the UK and the USA to regard employment law as intrusive and costly and there have been calls for deregulation. In Europe law is seen as important and there are fewer such calls. Good law should provide a clear framework and be proportionate to the problem it is seeking to address. It is important to see what law is really saying, rather than what others tell you it is saying.

Law varies from country to country in the nature of the rules themselves, how they are enforced and the remedies they provide. The rules and the principles for interpreting the rules are developed through legislation and decisions made by the courts. The latter are just as important as the former in setting the standards expected of employers.

The world's legal systems are divided broadly into two.

1 Systems dominated by legislation (codes, basic laws, statutes, acts, and so on), typical of Europe, South America, North Africa. In such systems law courts interpret and apply legislation.
2 Common law systems where case law and decisions made by law courts have a significant role, typical of Australia, Canada, Ireland, the UK, the USA and other British Commonwealth states. In these systems courts can develop new legal rules.

These traditions help to explain how some of the more innovative legal developments in, say, SMOKING AT WORK, REPETITIVE STRAIN INJURY, STRESS protection and BULLYING have arisen through test cases in common law jurisdictions. It also explains the UK's difficulties, which many feel exist, in absorbing EU employment law.

LAY OFF

During a downturn in business a company may decide to lay off some of its workers until conditions improve. Employees are not dismissed but their contracts of employment are temporarily suspended. To do this there must be either an express term or an implied term in the CONTRACT OF EMPLOYMENT. Alternatively, the employees must agree to being laid off. If they do not, they may have a claim for UNFAIR DISMISSAL or WRONGFUL DISMISSAL and/or REDUNDANCY payment and be entitled to COMPENSATION. In the USA the term lay off means DISMISSAL.

LEADERSHIP

The capacity to create a compelling vision, translate it into action and sustain it. Warren Bennis is one of the best-known management writers on leadership, and a man of many aphorisms: "Leadership is like beauty. It's hard to define, but you know it when you see it" and "Managers do things right, but Leaders do the right thing." Leadership was once thought in Europe to be synonymous with silver spoons, when qualities were defined as personality traits, hence the old adage that "leaders are born, not made". All psychologists now disagree with that statement. John Adair, a British writer and developer of ACTION CENTRED LEADERSHIP adds: "You cannot be taught Leadership. You must learn it for yourself."

Bennis offers four criteria for leadership.

1 A VISION that others can believe in and adopt as their own. "Vision is the art of seeing things invisible."
2 Communicating the vision and translating it into successful results. "The meaning of communication is its effect."
3 Trust. "The emotional glue that binds followers and leaders together."
4 Self-management. Persistence, commitment, integrity and challenge; a willingness to take risks; curiosity, passion and a willingness to continue learning, particularly from adversity and mistakes. "There is no such thing as failure, only feedback."

People you lead have to recognise that they too have power. The aim must be for people to say: "The leader did nothing – we did it ourselves."
Steve Shirley, president, FI Group

LEAN ORGANISATION

A modern term that has been linked with DOWNSIZING. It was initially used to describe organisations that achieved cost-effective production and service operations through flexible working, TEAM

WORK, self-development and EMPOWERMENT of both teams and individuals.

LEAVE

More than just HOLIDAY. Leave can be taken for a variety of reasons, such as maternity, paternity, JURY SERVICE or sickness, or it can be unauthorised. In the UK there is no statutory obligation to provide leave, nor generally does it have to be paid. Holiday and sick leave entitlement and payment arrangements should be detailed in an employee's CONTRACT OF EMPLOYMENT, or the STAFF HANDBOOK. Unauthorised leave, depending on the duration and the circumstances, may entitle an employer to start a DISCIPLINARY PROCEDURE against the individual concerned. (See also EXTENDED LEAVE; GARDEN LEAVE.)

LEC

Local Enterprise Council (see TRAINING AND ENTERPRISE COUNCILS).

LOCK-OUT

When employees are not allowed by their employer to work because they have been refused entry to the workplace or have been escorted from it. A lock-out usually occurs when an employer wants an unwilling workforce to accept specific changes in working methods, practices or terms and conditions. A lock-out suspends the employees' period of employment, but it does not break their CONTINUITY of employment. However, they may be dismissed at a later stage if they do not reach agreement with their employer.

LOWER EARNINGS LIMIT

The weekly level of earnings at which people have to start paying NATIONAL INSURANCE contributions and become entitled to certain social security BENEFITS. The limit usually changes each April in line with any cost of living increase.

MANAGERIAL HIERARCHIES

The analysis of bureaucratic administration, with each office subordinate to the one above it and each official's role determined by his office, was first undertaken by Max Weber in Germany. Alfred Chandler studied it further in the great American corporations, suggesting that the way an organisation operates is determined by its strategic goals. Tom Peters reckons that Chandler got it completely wrong, and that it is the structure of the organisation that determines the choices it makes about the markets it attacks. Peter Drucker thinks that it is neither chicken nor egg, but a circular process.

Weber's forecast at the turn of the century that hierarchical bureaucracies would become the major forces in commerce and industry came true. They were the common structure from 1900 to 1960, when their demolition accelerated. We are already seeing the truth of the predictions of Peter Drucker, Rosabeth Moss Kanter and Charles Handy that flat, non-hierarchical structures with empowered individuals and KNOWLEDGE WORKERS will predominate in future.

> *Management's job is to enable others; not to control them.*
> Ricardo Semler

MATERNITY RIGHTS

The rights to leave and BENEFITS of employees who become pregnant vary enormously from country to country with, broadly, the Nordic countries in Europe offering the most generous provisions. Rights can vary from two years' leave on full PAY after the birth to a few weeks' unpaid leave or SICK PAY.

With more and more women working, more and more people need time off work for maternity reasons. This is a fact that employers must accept and be sensitive to, regardless of the inconvenience (real or perceived) it causes. Organisations should anticipate and respond to such ABSENCE in a coherent and low-key way. Hostile or adverse treatment of a pregnant woman is SEXUAL DISCRIMINATION if it is connected with her pregnancy. Maternity also covers women who have recently given birth, including a woman returning to work after maternity leave or a new employee with a baby.

An organisation's maternity policy should:

- include a statement of the organisation's positive approach to maternity;
- be linked with other policies such as an EQUAL OPPORTUNITY policy;
- explain a woman's obligation to inform the organisation when she is, or suspects she might be, pregnant. This should stress the employer's responsibility for her HEALTH AND SAFETY and require her to co-operate with decisions to, say, redeploy her or change her terms of work temporarily in order to comply with the Management of Health and Safety at Work Regulations 1992;
- explain a woman's legal and occupational entitlements and what she needs to do to comply with them;
- identify the staff she needs to inform or consult;
- explain the options after she has given birth;
- outline what help or support the organisation provides to women with children, for example, subsidised childcare or a workplace creche;
- include a keep-in-touch strategy to reassure women on maternity leave that they will not be sidelined or got rid of.

The major legal rights are as follows.

1 Maternity leave

In the UK a woman is entitled to maternity leave during the later stages of pregnancy and after her child is born. Its duration depends on her length of service. For women with CONTINUOUS EMPLOYMENT of two years or more the period is up to 29 weeks after the birth and at least the six weeks before the expected birth. The basic entitlement for virtually all employees is 14 weeks, during which the employer need not pay REMUNERATION but other contractual rights continue and statutory maternity pay applies. Many employers are more generous. In all cases women have the right to return to their job, providing they comply with procedures, in particular the one that requires them to let the employer know when they intend to return.

A woman returning from maternity leave must receive any extra benefits or pay rises granted in her absence. If her job has changed or disappeared, she must be offered suitable alternative work; this means it has to be broadly comparable in terms of PAY, skill demands and status. However, employers are not entitled to shunt around someone returning from maternity leave simply because the replacement who filled in for her has turned out to be better at the job. The contract of the person providing cover should contain a clause saying that his or her contract will end when the woman on maternity leave returns.

There are complex rules covering maternity leave. Good advice is available from many sources, including the Equal Opportunities Commission, the Maternity Alliance, the Institute of Personnel and Development and the Department for Education and Employment. To refuse a full-time person a request to return part-time or job share will probably amount to DISCRIMINATION.

Maternity leave in other EU countries is often not as generous as in the UK, and women in the UK who have met the criteria for higher-rate payments also do reasonably well in European terms in maintaining their incomes. However, women in other EU countries with shorter qualifying periods of employment often do better than in the UK as maternity pay is closely integrated with sick pay. The 1994 directive on the protection of pregnant women at work provides for a minimum of 14 weeks' maternity leave. Longer leave entitlement in continental Europe is often integrated into PARENTAL LEAVE.

2 Maternity pay

PAY to cover maternity leave comes from two sources: the government and the employer. In recent years the burden has moved from the former to the latter. In the UK all women on maternity leave qualify for Statutory Maternity Pay (SMP) for 18 weeks. For those with two years' service or more the employer must top this up with nine-tenths of six weeks' normal pay. Many organisations provide a further top-up of, say, half pay for three months. It is a benefit that can be attractive to job applicants and to current employees who might otherwise leave. These entitlements should be widely advertised, especially in RECRUITMENT literature. Family-friendly firms are fashionable nowadays.

MEDICAL EXAMINATION

An organisation may make a job subject to the prospective employee having a medical examination. This usually happens in businesses where safety is an issue, such as transport, or where the individual is applying for a senior job. The examination may take a variety of forms. In the USA testing for DRUGS and alcohol is becoming increasingly common.

Employers can require employees to undergo a medical examination if they:

- have been absent from work for several weeks;
- have taken intermittent sick leave;
- have an injury or ILLNESS that may affect their work.

The requirement for such examinations is often written into the CONTRACT OF EMPLOYMENT. Employees have to be asked to give their permission and can refuse. The examination may be carried out by the organisation's doctor, a doctor engaged specifically for the examination or the employee's own doctor or consultant. It is paid for by the employer. An organisation may decide to give certain managers, among their BENEFITS, the opportunity to have regular medical examinations at the organisation's expense.

MEDICAL RECORD
See HEALTH RECORD.

MEDICAL REPORT
An organisation may ask a doctor to review an employee's medical condition or ask the employee for permission to contact his or her own doctor for a medical report. Employers must comply with the conditions of the Access to Medical Reports Act 1988 (see HEALTH RECORD).

MENTOR
A mentor is different from a coach. If a manager is COACHING an employee there will be occasions when the employee wants to ask a question, or to ask for help, yet feels that the coach is not the right person. This is when a mentor can help. The mentor should be at least at the same level as the coach, and is often at a higher level, and should have considerable relevant experience. The mentor's role is personal. When necessary, he or she can hear both sides of a story to resolve problems.

MINIMUM WAGE
A minimum wage can be set by statute or collective agreement. In Europe three methods are used.

1 National statutory minimum wage
France, Luxembourg, the Netherlands, Portugal and Spain have a national statutory minimum wage. In Belgium and Greece a national minimum is established by collective agreement. Sometimes there are lower rates for young workers. The UK will have a statutory minimum wage under the programme of the new Labour government.

2 Collectively agreed sectoral minimum
Austria, Denmark, Finland, Germany, Italy and Sweden pay a minimum that is set by sectoral COLLECTIVE BARGAINING. However, the way the agree-

ments operate and the coverage of the workforce vary. For example, in Italy and Austria sectoral agreements are effectively binding on all employees in an industry; in Finland the agreement is binding on non-signatory firms based on levels of union membership in the industrial sector.

3 Regulated minimum

In Ireland a binding minimum is set through Joint Labour Committees or negotiated via Joint Industrial Councils for sectors with low union density or low pay. These arrangements cover around 10% of the workforce. In the UK wages councils, which set the minimum rate for unorganised sectors, exist only for agriculture.

MISCONDUCT

Behaviour that an employer considers unacceptable and may result in a DISCIPLINARY PROCEDURE. Misconduct ranges from acts such as stealing, which usually entitle the employer to dismiss the guilty employee on the spot, to minor transgressions such as unauthorised LATENESS or failure to wear the proper uniform, which may merit only a warning unless the misconduct is persistent. Every CONTRACT OF EMPLOYMENT should include details of an organisation's rules of conduct and disciplinary procedures, or should indicate where they can be found. If there is a STAFF HANDBOOK, it is good practice to include some examples of behaviour that the company considers to be misconduct, especially in grey areas such as BAD LANGUAGE, DRESS, and so on.

MISSION STATEMENT

There is no single definition of a mission statement, but it can be described as "the enduring purpose of an organisation or an individual". A mission statement should describe the attitudes and expectations of an organisation. It may describe a company's intentions regarding:

- competition;
- technological advance;

- product quality;
- commitment to employees;
- its role in society.

The statement gives a view of the overall strategy of an organisation. It is often used as a public statement of a company's values and expectations.

> *I know you believe you understand what you think I said, but how do you know that what you heard was what I meant.*
> Anon

MITBESTIMMUNG

Literally meaning co-determination, *Mitbestimmung* is a term used to describe Germany's various statutory systems for employee information, CONSULTATION and involvement in decision-making. These have various strands. Probably the best known, but least influential on a day-to-day basis, is employee representation on the supervisory boards (*Aufsichtsrat*) of companies. Supervisory boards appoint the management board (*Vorstand*) and monitor overall policy, including the annual report and accounts. In smaller companies with 500–2,000 employees this is one-third representation; in companies with more than 2,000 employees the supervisory board consists of equal numbers of employee and shareholder members, although the chair (who is elected by the shareholders) has a casting vote in the event of a tie, and managers (who usually support the shareholders) also have separate representation within the employee camp. In large companies in the coal, iron and steel industries (the so-called Montan industries), there is also 50:50 representation, but the chair is neutral and the director of human resources cannot be appointed without the agreement of the employee members.

More important for day-to-day management is the structure of elected works councils. These may be set up, if the employees choose, in any establishment with five or more workers. In practice this happens in larger firms: around two-thirds of all private-sector employees work in a company with a WORKS COUNCIL. TRADE UNION REPRESENTATIVES account for about two-thirds of all elected works council members. They have extensive rights to information, consultation and, on certain issues, co-determination. This means, in the narrow sense, that the employer cannot proceed with an action without the agreement of the works council, or if it refuses, the decision of an independent ARBITRATION panel. The issues include the organisation of WORKING TIME, HEALTH AND SAFETY, job design, company BENEFITS, the hiring, transfer and regrading of workers, and the right to negotiate on severance schemes.

MOBILITY

The idea that the job is the thing, not where it is done; in other words, the right of an employer to require employees to work somewhere other than the place at which they were originally employed to work. Employers who want mobility from their employees must ensure that it is clearly set out in their CONTRACT OF EMPLOYMENT. The degree of mobility required must also be specified; for example, a contract that refers to a move within the same town may not cover a move to a greenfield site. Employers cannot fire employees for refusing to move if their contract of employment does not include a mobility clause.

MOONLIGHTING

Having a second job in addition to your main job. What people do in their spare time is, of course, up to them, but a CONTRACT OF EMPLOYMENT can forbid an employee to moonlight. Even if it does not, employers are unlikely to want to continue to employ someone whose performance is substandard because they are continually tired from doing two jobs. Moonlighting poses other potential problems for those who engage in it. For example, employees who call in sick when they are simply tired or have been held up at the other job may be guilty of criminal fraud in falsely claiming SICK PAY. They may also be moonlighting for a rival organisation.

MOTIVATIONAL FACTORS

The label given by Frederick Herzberg to those factors which his research found to be motivational. The dissatisfaction factors are better known (see HYGIENE FACTORS).

NATIONAL INSURANCE

Many governments impose a tax on income that has another name to make it sound more nobly intentioned. The justification is that payment of this tax entitles people to BENEFITS – a state pension, for example – that payment of ordinary income tax does not. In the UK most working people between 16 and pension age must pay National Insurance contributions (NICs). If they have not been credited with enough of the right class of contributions at the right time, they do not qualify for sickness benefit, invalidity benefit, maternity allowance, retirement pension, widow's benefit or JOBSEEKER'S ALLOWANCE.

Contributions are ranked as follows.

- Class 1: paid by people who work for an employer.
- Class 2: paid by people who are SELF-EMPLOYED.
- Class 3: voluntary contributions.
- Class 4: paid in addition to Class 2 contributions by self-employed people whose profits or gains are above a certain limit in any one tax year.

NEGLIGENCE

If people suffer damage or injury as a result of an organisation's failure to take reasonable care they can sue the organisation for negligence. All organisations should be adequately insured against claims by employees, visitors or others for a wide range of eventualities. An increasing number of types of injuries are being successfully claimed for, including post-traumatic stress disorder (PTSD) and REPETITIVE STRAIN INJURY (RSI).

NETWORK

A fashionable word in some organisations, and not just for computers. Organisations have always contained informal networks, but with the advent of flexible working practices some have seen the need to formalise these for the benefit of the business. External networks also exist with suppliers, customers and so on (see PARTNERING). Some of these may also need to be formalised to ensure the smooth running of a business.

NEURO-LINGUISTIC PROGRAMMING

When we interpret the world around us we do it in our own preferred style. Neuro-linguistic programming (NLP) describes the way in which we prefer to filter and process our experiences through our senses – the neuro bit; the way in which we interpret our experiences through language – the linguistic bit; and the way we code language and behaviour into our own personal style – the programming bit. Some people think in pictures and speak using visually descriptive words: "I've got the picture. I see what you mean." Others are more sensuous and relate to feelings: "I can't put my finger on it, but I've got a bad feeling about it." The third group comprises listeners and readers who find the spoken or written word more expressive: "I hear what you're saying and it rings a bell."

NLP teaches us that we are all different, and that if we wish to communicate we will be more effective if we adapt to the style of the recipient. We also filter our experiences in different ways. To some a half-empty glass is a half-full glass; to some change is fearful and to others it is a challenge; some see the differences between things and others point out the similarities. These filters affect our beliefs and our outlook on the world. NLP can help us identify our current style, and modify our behaviour to achieve more of what we want. NLP is not about learning new skills; it is about improving the quality of understanding.

NIGHT WORK

Organisations that require people to work at night usually operate a SHIFT WORK system and may pay those on the night shift more than those on the day shift. Shift workers often alternate between night, evening and day shifts, which can cause problems for those who have difficulty adapting their domestic and sleeping arrangements. It is therefore good practice to allow a trial period for employees who have never worked shifts to see how they adapt. In the UK children cannot, with the exception of stage performances and such like, be employed before 7am or after 7pm.

The EU's Working Time Directive 1993 (operative since November 1996) defines night work as any period of not less than seven hours which must include the hours between midnight and 5am. Night workers are people at least 3 hours of whose working time takes place at night time. They should not work more than an average of eight hours in any 24-hour period. If the work involves "special hazards or heavy physical or mental strain", which should be defined by collective or other agreements or national legislation, they can never work more than eight hours. Night workers are entitled to a free health check when starting their job and at regular intervals thereafter. If they develop a health problem connected with their night work they have the right to be transferred to suitable day work.

NLP
See NEURO-LINGUISTIC PROGRAMMING.

NOTICE
Employees who have been employed for at least one month must give at least seven days' notice if they want to quit. Under the Employment Rights Act 1996, all employees are free to leave their jobs, providing that they give their employer the notice specified in their CONTRACT OF EMPLOYMENT and observe any other restrictive clauses.

Problems can occur when an employee storms out after a row using words that could imply resignation. If a dispute arises, an INDUSTRIAL TRIBUNAL is likely to regard an employer who assumes an employee has resigned as having dismissed that employee. In most cases, when an employer terminates a contract of employment, with or without notice, it is known as DISMISSAL. The employer must follow a fair procedure or the employee may claim UNFAIR DISMISSAL.

The statutory minimum notice period for an employee who has worked continuously for an employer for more than one month but less than two years is one week. After two years of CONTINUOUS EMPLOYMENT it increases by one week for each complete year, up to a maximum of 12 weeks after 12 years' employment. Under the Employment Protection (Part-time Employees) Regulations 1995, a part-time worker is entitled to receive the same notice as a full-time worker.

Mandatory notice periods, set by law or collective agreement, in many continental European countries have been and, for the most part, continue to be longer than in the UK. They can extend up to several months or in excess of a year in the case of long-service employees. In many instances, such as in Germany and Belgium, this simply serves to ensure that individual employees receive a reasonable pay-off on termination of employment through PAY in lieu of notice.

NOTICE OF INDUSTRIAL ACTION

In the UK an employer must be given seven days' notice of lawful INDUSTRIAL ACTION, that is, action in pursuance of a legitimate dispute following a BALLOT (of which the employer is also entitled to seven days' notice). Failure by a TRADE UNION to comply with any of the notice procedures entitles an employer to take out an INJUNCTION and/or claim COMPENSATION from the union.

OBJECTIVES

Targets for the future, not day-to-day activities. Objectives are milestones for managing change, not procedures for sustaining the status quo. They are specific aims to deliver an organisation's strategy. Objectives should be SMART:

- Specific
- Measurable
- Agreed
- Realistic
- Timeframed

OCCUPATIONAL BENEFITS

See BENEFITS; FLEXIBLE BENEFITS.

OCCUPATIONAL HEALTH PRACTITIONER

As knowledge of health risks at work increases and the legal duties of employers become more demanding they are increasingly turning to the occupational health practitioner (OHP). Particular areas of concern are musculo-skeletal problems of all sorts, eye problems and STRESS. Most employers are now required and/or choose to undertake extensive health monitoring. Some important questions are as follows.

- Should a specialist be directly employed by the organisation or contracted when required?
- What is the relationship between the organisation, the worker and the practitioner?
- Are there issues of confidentiality?
- Are there adequate professional standards in the various practitioner groups?

The advantage of in-house practitioners (such as eye specialists, physiotherapists or generalists in occupational health) is that they should know the nature and demands of work in the organisation. But they may be expensive to provide. If skills are bought in, the role and scope of the practitioner and instructions on dealing with employees must be clearly defined as part of the process of ensuring acceptable standards of care and competence.

Confidentiality is a complex matter. If, however, everyone involved is aware of the purposes of checks, monitoring, and so on, employees are unlikely to object to the OHP providing information to the employer.

OCCUPATIONAL PENSION
See PENSIONS.

OUTPLACEMENT
A word that grew out of the fashion for DOWNSIZING to describe programmes designed to help employees facing REDUNDANCY get another job or make some other kind of career change. The programmes are usually provided by specialist consultants and funded by employers, which means that they may be treated as a taxable benefit. Some companies have developed their own internal outplacement services when large-scale redundancies have been announced. The advantage is that the people running such services know the employees and the industry. The disadvantage is that they may be viewed by outplaced individuals as being insufficiently independent and out of touch with other industries or the current job market. A basic outplacement programme may include any or all of the following.

- Help with producing a CV.
- Assessment of potential.
- Help in identifying prospective employers.
- Identification of training courses for PERSONAL DEVELOPMENT or career change.
- Help with self-presentational skills, including letter writing and interview technique (perhaps using video recording and playback).
- Counselling and support in managing the change, including its effects on family and finances.

Some outplacement consultancies make considerable efforts to find suitable jobs for their clients and maintain databases on the unadvertised job market (which, in the UK, is estimated to account for 60–70% of all jobs). Outplacement programmes can also be tailored to the needs of those considering a major career change, which may involve retraining or setting up a business.

> *How would I describe managing subcontractors? Simple. Crisis management.*
> NHA manager, Report to ILO, 1995

OUTSOURCING

A growing trend in recent years has been to outsource for skills, for example, to a subcontractor or employment agency. The process requires careful analysis. Some useful questions are as follows.

- Is the function which it is proposed to outsource for appropriate for outsourcing? Are there risks to confidentiality, quality, consistency of delivery and, perhaps, of demotivating in-house staff?
- Are there potential HEALTH AND SAFETY problems?
- Are the staff to be supplied by the subcontractor or agency well trained, skilled and reliable?
- Are there sufficient good quality and reliable subcontractors and agencies?
- What are the costs of devising specifications, tendering, selecting, liaising with and managing subcontractors or AGENCY STAFF?

Clearly, there are many circumstances where using a subcontractor and/or agency makes sense, especially where the skill is specialised or the need is short-term. But there may be others where an employer should think carefully before outsourcing.

OVERPAYMENT OF WAGES

If an employer has overpaid an employee the money can usually be recovered. It may not be if the employer has misunderstood the law or has misled the employee into believing he was entitled to the money, or the employee has varied his standard of living in good faith and without knowing of his employer's claim. In recovering an overpayment an employer should ensure that the number and amount of deductions made from future WAGES do not place an unfair burden on the employee.

OVERSEAS WORK

A growing number of people now work outside their home countries as a result of the globalisation of business and the open market for jobs in the European Union. However, there are also trends towards using local people in multinational organisations and developing their management skills. Organisations that send people to work abroad should take steps to ensure that the adjustment is smooth. Failure to do this may result in below-par performance from the employee. The following should be considered.

- **PAY** Does it need to be adjusted because of a higher cost of living? If so, is it better to give a percentage rise or for the organisation to pay some of the costs directly; for example, housing.
- **CULTURE and language** What preparation do employees need? An intensive language course plus a programme of cultural initiation may be necessary simply to be able to do the job. Business methods and etiquette can differ substantially from one country to another. This is particularly true for countries like Japan.
- **The family** What particular problems may employees' spouses face and how can the organisation help? This is particularly relevant in Islamic countries. What about schooling for the children?
- **Health** What are the health risks and what should be done about them?
- **Safety** Are there any particular dangers,

such as a high crime rate or political unrest?
- **Social contact**   What arrangements need to be put in place so that, in the initial period especially, employees and their families do not feel isolated?

OVERTIME

Hours worked over and beyond the standard working week for the employee. Overtime may be a contractual requirement, with the CONTRACT OF EMPLOYMENT defining the hours to be worked beyond the standard working week. Most EU countries, with the exception of the UK, control the incidence of overtime working by LAW, by collective agreement or by official intervention. As a result, overtime working, and hence overall hours worked, tends to be lower in continental Europe than in the UK, which has the longest average hours actually worked in the European Union.

People working overtime may be paid extra or given time off in lieu. The latter is now a requirement in many sectors of the German economy, where unions and employers have sought to curb overtime working in an effort to stimulate job creation. Payment may vary depending on whether the work was carried out on a weekday, at the weekend or on a PUBLIC HOLIDAY. Managers, especially senior ones, are often expected to put in the hours it takes to do their job without extra payment.

Parallel thinking

We are currently taught that critical analysis will solve our problems, a thinking system bequeathed us by the Greeks. *You feel a sharp pain when you sit down. You examine the chair and find a pin. You remove the pin and the problem is solved.* The method is simple and it works well – when there is a simple or a single cause. But many of our problems do not have a single cause, or have causes which we do not yet know how to remove.

Edward De Bono suggests that this traditional thinking process is negative, judgemental and adversarial in its approach. We remove the 'untruths' to seek 'the truth'. We like certainty – the single answer, because we dislike the uncertainty of optional possible solutions. We have become good at proving others to be wrong. Worse, it is a process which demands factual information from our knowledge bank and ignores creativity.

What is needed, states De Bono, is a creative thinking process that reserves judgement, and seeks to create parallel possibilities from which to design a way forward out of the problem. De Bono calls it "parallel thinking", the very nature of which means, he says, "that there can be no single or simple definition of the concept." (See also LATERAL THINKING.)

Parental leave

Most European countries, apart from the UK, have some form of statutory or agreed provision for parental leave, allowing either parent to take time off work after maternity leave or, where applicable, paternity leave has expired to care for a young child. An EU directive, which was created out of an agreement between the SOCIAL PARTNERS under the SOCIAL CHAPTER and will apply to the UK after the abandonment of the opt-out, requires employers to grant three months' unpaid LEAVE to either parent. Leave must be taken before the child is eight years old, although countries can set lower cut-off points.

National arrangements are often more generous than the directive. In Germany either parent can remain at home until the child is three. Parents can swap over during the leave, and there is a means-tested state benefit for part of the leave.

In practice leave is overwhelmingly taken by women, although in Sweden there is official encouragement for men to participate. Swedish law also allows leave to be extended until the child is eight if it is taken on a part-time basis.

PARTICIPATIVE MANAGEMENT

One of the four management styles identified by Rensis Likert.

System 1: Exploitative authoritarian Management by fear and coercion, where decision-making is at the top only, communication is top-down, and superiors and subordinates are psychologically far apart.

System 2: Benevolent authoritarian Management by carrot, but with no stick. Subordinates are still basically subservient, and what information does flow up is only what the boss is thought to want to hear.

System 3: Consultative Communication flows both ways, but management takes the decisions.

System 4: Participative Management is concerned to get employees involved in groups capable of making decisions. Challenging goals are set to encourage high performance. Communication flows easily in all directions. Decision-making is a participative process.

Likert maintained that research showed System 4 achieved the best results for the company. Inefficient units were invariably managed by System 1 job-centred managers, who kept their subordinates busy working in prescribed ways using tight time standards. Managers of high-performing units were employee-centred, listing their main tasks as helping to develop their staff and build a TEAM. They were more concerned with the overall target than with individual methods. They also encouraged maximum participation in decision-making.

PARTNERING

Another fashionable word to describe companies that concentrate on their CORE BUSINESS but work closely with their suppliers to ensure that they get the quality of materials and components they need to make their products. (Contrast with VERTICAL INTEGRATION.)

PART-TIME WORK

Part-time employment has been the major area of employment growth throughout Europe during the 1990s. One in seven people in the European Union is working part-time. In the mid-1990s part-time work was highest in the Netherlands and the UK and lowest in Greece, Portugal, Spain and Italy. Just under one-quarter of the UK workforce was part-time, compared with one-sixth in 1973, with the fastest growth in part-time work coming between 1973 and 1992. Part-time jobs are likely to continue to grow in the UK and elsewhere as companies, especially in the services sector and most notably in retailing, attempt to adjust their work schedules to customers' demands. Although 75–85% of part-time workers are women, men now account for a gently rising proportion of the total in almost all countries.

Definitions and treatment of part-time workers vary around the world. In most European countries employment rights, such as maternity leave, apply irrespective of the hours worked. In the UK, the Netherlands, Norway and Ireland employees who work less than a defined minimum number of hours are excluded from certain employment rights. An exemption from NATIONAL INSURANCE contributions applies below a specified income level in Denmark, Germany, Ireland and the UK. However, part-time workers' employment rights and protection have improved owing to legislation, especially in the European Union. They must now, broadly, receive pro-rata rights and BENEFITS of full-timers.

It is a mistake for employers to assume that part-timers are working only for pin money or to prevent boredom, are more prone to ABSENCE and

ILLNESS (they are not), or do not want a career or training. As the legal rights of part-timers are now in line with those of full-timers, it is expected that employers will increasingly bring their occupational rights and benefits into line as well.

Pay

What people receive for the job they do. Pay can be determined by individual negotiation or with reference to company norms, local industry rates or national collective agreements. It is not just the money people get; it also includes BENEFITS such as company cars and contributions made towards PENSIONS. The term "basic pay", however, commonly refers to the cash element, excluding any bonuses or allowances. Whereas in the UK less than half of the workforce now have their basic pay set by COLLECTIVE BARGAINING, in continental Europe national or industry-level negotiations still embrace 70–90% of the labour force, depending on the country. National or industry agreements provide a floor, with additional top-ups of as much as 30–40% negotiated at company-level or set unilaterally by the employer.

Since the 1980s organisations have increasingly recognised that pay bills are an overhead that can determine whether a company survives or not. Initiatives such as PERFORMANCE-RELATED PAY and PROFIT-RELATED PAY were introduced to encourage employees to contribute to the success of the company by allowing them a share of the financial rewards.

Pay in Lieu of Notice

A CONTRACT OF EMPLOYMENT may be written to give an employer the right to insist that someone who has been dismissed or who has resigned leaves the organisation without working out their period of NOTICE in return for the WAGES they would have received if they had done so. The payment should be the gross amount due to the employee less deductions for PAYE and NATIONAL INSURANCE contributions, but pay in lieu of notice paid as compensation for immediate DISMISSAL is tax free (subject to a limit of

£30,000, inclusive of any non-contractual REDUNDANCY or lump-sum severance payments), and PAYE deductions do not have to be made. In cases of redundancy pay in lieu of notice can be given, but there may be legal difficulties if dates of dismissal are subject to consultation periods.

PAYE

The acronym for Pay As You Earn. A PAYE income tax system operates in the UK. It requires employers to deduct tax from payments made to employees and forward the money to the Inland Revenue. The employer has to provide the Inland Revenue with details of all financial transactions between the employer and employee. Each employee has a PAYE code that reflects their tax allowances for the appropriate tax year. This ensures that the correct amount of tax is deducted from an employee's earnings.

PENSIONS

There are two types of pension schemes commonly operated by companies for their employees: final salary pension schemes, also called defined benefit schemes; and money purchase personal pension schemes, also called defined contribution schemes. The Pensions Act 1995, which came into force in April 1997, brought the UK into line with best practice in other countries. It made substantial changes to the rights of employees in relation to company schemes, commonly called occupational pension schemes. The act included measures to ensure sex equality in occupational schemes, and set up the Occupational Pensions Regulatory Authority (OPRA) to regulate and control such schemes. The pension scheme must have a bank account separate from the company bank account, and the actuary, auditor and fund manager appointed to oversee the scheme must be completely independent. Additional safeguards have included the extension of the role of the pensions ombudsman to adjudicate in cases of disputes and complaints of maladministration. Occupational schemes can no longer be a condition of employment; employees have the right to choose a personal pension instead of their employer's scheme.

In the UK some companies have contracted in to the government State Earnings Related Pension Scheme (SERPS), some have contracted out, and others have single schemes that allow employees to choose whether to contract in or out. SERPS was introduced in the Social Security Pensions Act 1975 and started on April 6th 1978 to provide a pension of 1.25% of an individual's average annual revalued band earnings for each year completed after April 1978 up to a maximum of 25% by 1998. (Revalued band earnings are earnings between the lower and upper earnings limits for NATIONAL INSURANCE contributions. The lower limit is approximately equal to one-quarter of national average earnings, and the upper limit is about one-and-three-quarters of national average earnings.) SERPS is on top of the basic state pension.

The 1975 act allowed approved occupational pension schemes to contract out of SERPS. This meant that the scheme undertook to provide benefits at least equal to a guaranteed minimum pension (GMP) in place of a SERPS pension, in return for a reduction in employer and employee National Insurance contributions. An individual's GMP is calculated in a similar way to the SERPS pension. The requirement for occupational schemes that have contracted out of SERPS to guarantee a minimum pension ended in April 1997. However, occupational scheme pensions must still be increased each year in line with the Retail Price Index (RPI) or by 5%, whichever is the lesser, in respect of deferred members. These are people who have left the company but have retained benefits in the scheme. With the increased administrative procedures and costs involved, few insurance companies are now offering contracted-out schemes. Many companies are in the process of converting their current schemes to contracted-in only.

How to choose an appropriate pension is still a conundrum for the average employee. Many companies now offer a pensions advice day when expert advisers are available to help employees.

PERFORMANCE-RELATED PAY

Employees' PAY that depends partly on their performance. This type of pay can take many forms and may or may not be linked to a performance APPRAISAL system. Performance-related pay can be based on individual, TEAM or company performance, or any combination thereof. The overall objective is to improve the performance of the organisation and reward employees for their achievement.

There is little research to confirm that performance-related pay has a positive effect on motivation but, in theory, such schemes force management to pay greater attention to measuring performance. The real skill, however, is in determining the performance criteria that trigger the extra payments, which should be challenging yet reasonable and fair. There is no point in setting a target over which an employee has little or no influence or one that is impossible to achieve. Similarly, setting short-term financial targets may lead to long-term interests being ignored.

Performance-related pay has implications for trade unions and other staff associations. As payment levels are determined by the individual's performance, the role of the union is to influence the design of the scheme and to support employees in any dispute. It is the most common form of variable pay in Europe and the USA. In most countries it is used to remunerate managers, professional and technical staff, and to a lesser extent operatives and support staff. However, in Germany managers are less likely to be covered by this type of scheme, and in Sweden mainly manual workers are covered. Within the European Union performance-related pay is most widely used in Portugal.

PERSONAL DEVELOPMENT

Organisations are increasingly encouraging their employees to take responsibility for their own development, while attempting to provide the motivation, and in some cases the financial support, to do so. Support can be provided by:

- helping to define the individual's career direction;
- providing a coach or MENTOR;
- advising on appropriate academic or professional courses;
- allocating projects that will develop expertise and or experience;
- seconding the individual to another part of the organisation.

PERSONAL HYGIENE
A lack of this can be embarrassing. There are a few jobs where poor hygiene standards are illegal, for example, handling food and working in health-care. Standards in these sectors must be kept high, helped by the provision of adequate hygiene facilities and enforced by strict disciplinary rules. Outside these special areas employers should handle sensitively situations where employees have poor hygiene standards and cause offence. People may not be aware of the problem or they may have a rare medical condition that requires medical treatment. Occupational health practitioners should be able to give advice.

PLACE OF WORK
Employees must be told their place of work in their STATEMENT OF TERMS OF WORK. It can be, for example, "21 High Street, Mudtown", or "any of the company's offices in the UK", or "your home", although you may be required to attend any of the company's PREMISES from time to time. It is worth linking this information with MOBILITY clauses.

PORTFOLIO WORK
The future of today's KNOWLEDGE WORKERS, who without the prospect of long-term careers in one organisation divide their lives into several areas of work. Charles Handy believes portfolio working has the potential to enhance the PERSONAL DEVELOPMENT and quality of life of every individual.

William Bridges, in his book *Jobshift*, offers clear guidelines on how to do it.

POSITIVE DISCRIMINATION

Originally developed in the USA and sometimes referred to as AFFIRMATIVE ACTION, this is DISCRIMINATION in favour of an individual on the grounds of race, sex or marital status. It results in discrimination against someone else on the same grounds, which is unlawful in many countries. You can welcome or encourage applicants who are women or who belong to an ethnic minority, but you cannot give them preference. Exceptions are sometimes made with the aim of promoting the interests of groups considered to be at a disadvantage. For example, in the UK the Race Relations Act and the Sex Discrimination Act allow limited positive discrimination on the grounds of race or sex in respect of the provision of training.

PREMISES

Employers have a duty under the Occupiers Liability Act 1957, the Defective Premises Act 1972 and the Workplace (Health, Safety and Welfare) Regulations 1992 to ensure that their premises are safe for occupation. They are also responsible for the safety of all employees and visitors to the premises.

PRIVATE LIFE

Is the private life of staff the legitimate concern of their employer? The answer is usually no, but there may be circumstances where private activities, especially of a criminal or sexual nature, can cause concern and reflect badly on an organisation. Many organisations state what their expectations of staff are in the CONTRACT OF EMPLOYMENT. Unnecessary intrusion is unacceptable, but legitimate concerns are acceptable; for example, if a school teacher is dealing in child pornography, or a manager with access to information valuable to a competitor is having an affair with a manager of that competitor.

Probation period

The initial trial period often given to a new employee – nothing to do with a criminal act. Employers use probationary periods to give them time to assess whether they have chosen the right person. For example, does the employee have the skills claimed in the application form and at the interview as well as an attitude appropriate to the CULTURE of the organisation? A probationary period also allows new employees to see if the job is what it was made out to be and whether the organisation is one in which they will be happy.

Many employers see probation as a civilised way of allowing them to dispense with new employees who prove to be unsuitable. However, those who write a probationary period into a CONTRACT OF EMPLOYMENT may fall foul of anti-DISCRIMINATION and EQUAL OPPORTUNITY legislation, unless they clearly define what the recruit must achieve to be considered suitable. A better option is to employ people initially on short-term contracts, which define the personal QUALIFICATIONS that must be attained if the worker is to be offered a permanent post at the end of the short-term contract.

Opponents of probationary periods claim that they should not be necessary if job interviews are properly conducted. They also point out that, in practice, the absence of a probationary period does not prevent either an employer or an employee giving NOTICE if things are not working out.

Profit-related pay

Part of an employees' PAY that is based on the profit the organisation makes. In the UK the profit-related element of employees' pay, in schemes that satisfy the requirements of tax legislation and are registered with the Inland Revenue, gets favourable tax treatment, although this is being phased out. The percentage of profit to be allocated for profit-related pay (PRP) must be set before the start of the scheme. Individuals can receive up to 20% of their annual pay tax free up to a maximum of £4,000. From January 1st 1998 the maximum will be £2,000; in 1999 it will be £1,000;

and in 2000 tax-free PRP schemes will be abolished. One argument against such schemes is that under the rules companies are required to give every employee in the scheme a share of the bonus regardless of whether they have been excellent or poor performers. This is why many companies prefer bonus schemes that can be more directly based on the contribution an employee has made (see PERFORMANCE-RELATED PAY).

PROTECTIVE EQUIPMENT

Where employees are at risk at work from hazardous substances (chemical, biological – viruses, bacteria, and so on), from other human beings or even from animals they must be protected. Manufacturers of protective equipment such as gloves, masks, spats, hearing protectors, protective creams and goggles have ensured that virtually every risk has its recommended equipment. The bad news for employers is that they have to provide it free, keep it up to date and well maintained, and train staff in its use.

PROTESTANT WORK ETHIC

Articulated by Max Weber at the turn of the century. Weber, a devout Calvinist, firmly believed in the 19th-century ethic that man was created to work and that sloth would be rewarded with damnation. But Weber's more interesting work was to identify and promote the hierarchical bureaucracy management style, a structure that suited the era, motivated managers and spread rapidly throughout the world as the best way to run an organisation.

PRP

See PROFIT-RELATED PAY.

PSYCHOLOGICAL CONTRACT

A term coined by Edgar Schein to denote what employees expect from employers, in terms of both PAY and how they will be developed. This unwritten contract also includes an employer's expectations about the loyalty and diligence of the people who work for it. (See also CAREER ANCHORS; CULTURE.)

PSYCHOMETRIC TESTING

Intelligence, temperament, behavioural and personality tests devised by occupational psychologists for personnel selection, vocational guidance and personal development. The purpose of psychometric testing is to help predict CAPABILITY and how someone will fit into the company CULTURE, and to identify individual qualities and characteristics that the company would like to see developed or modified.

There are some 200 personality tests in use, most of which were developed for the USA. Because cultural and ethnic differences influence responses to them, psychologists question the usefulness of many of the tests. Some psychologists are also concerned that companies are using personality tests in the recruitment process. These are really designed to monitor development; ability and aptitude tests should be used for recruitment.

The British Psychological Society publishes an evaluation review of all the tests available in the UK. Level A Review lists the ability tests and Level B Review lists the personality tests.

PUBLIC HOLIDAY

A statutory general holiday. Public holidays vary from country to country. If the holiday falls on a Saturday or Sunday it is usually transferred to a weekday. A public or bank holiday does not give an employee a legal right to a paid holiday in the UK. Holiday entitlements form part of an employee's CONTRACT OF EMPLOYMENT and therefore an individual's right to whether they are allowed to take the public holiday, have a day in lieu, or get paid extra for working on a public holiday.

QUALIFICATIONS

Not merely certificates that indicate a certain level of educational, vocational, technical or other attainment, but whatever skills you need to do a job. A job specification should define the required inputs, processes and outputs. The inputs are what the job holder needs to know and be able to do. The process defines how the job holder applies the knowledge and skill to do the work; that is, the behavioural requirements, such as a need to be articulate, or methodical or able to plan and prioritise. The outputs are the objective that the job holder is expected to achieve. Thus both inputs and processes will identify the required qualifications.

Before advertising a job, an employer should think about and then clearly define what qualifications are required and avoid overstating them. Setting an unrealistically high target for candidates will mean fewer applicants and, worse, dissatisfaction among recruits when they find their talents are not used.

QUALIFYING PERIOD

The length of service, for example, four weeks, two months or two years, that may affect an employee's entitlement to many employment rights, for example, for UNFAIR DISMISSAL or REDUNDANCY. The Employment Rights Act 1996 specifies the qualifying periods. Increasingly, especially in the European Union, no qualifying period is necessary; employment rights exist from the day a person starts a job. An example now is the UK Sunday Trading Act 1994, which prevents employees who refuse to work on Sundays from being fired. (See also CONTINUITY.)

QUALITY CIRCLE

A group of employees at all levels of an organisation who meet on a regular basis to discuss and make recommendations on, for example, changes to working practices and resolving work problems. The decisions or recommendations made can result in changes in job structure, its component parts and any aspect of work that affects productivity and quality. Quality circles started in Japan and are an important part of the Japanese system of management. They took off in the USA during the 1970s, and by 1983 some 6,200 sites were operating quality circles. However, during the 1990s quality circles have fallen out of favour in the USA and Europe. Many programmes have been abandoned or failed because of:

- insufficient management support;
- inadequate leader preparation and/or member training;
- poor internal publicity;
- failure to involve unions and/or middle management;
- poor management response to quality circle recommendations;
- the selection of inappropriate problems for consideration by the quality circle.

QUALITY MANAGEMENT

How production faults can be eliminated by a management-led philosophy of CONTINUOUS IMPROVEMENT in every process from planning through production to customer service. It was first adopted by the Japanese after the second world war following the teaching of W. Edwards Deming and Joseph Juran. Both Deming and Juran worked in Japan for a long time before recognition came in their own country.

> *Most re-engineering efforts fail or fall short of their mark because of the absence of trust – meaning respect for the individual, his or her goodwill, intelligence and native, but long shackled curiosity.*
> Tom Peters, 1993

QUALITY OF WORKING LIFE

The simple idea that if people feel good about their working conditions they are likely to be more productive. This can be achieved in many ways but probably needs to start with employee involvement in the decision-making processes that effect their work. Increasing focus has been put on the quality of working life in many countries, including the USA where a more behavioural approach to employment has begun to change the traditional adversarial relationship between management and unions.

R

RACE
This should be distinguished from nationality, ethnicity and RELIGION. UK LAW bans DISCRIMINATION on the grounds of race and nationality but not religion. Most developed economies have laws banning racial and related discrimination. Other legal systems ban religious discrimination and some ban ethnic discrimination. Some have no rules at all. In the European Union nationals of member states are free to move from one state to another. They must not be treated less favourably than home nationals.

REASONABLENESS
In employment matters decisions must usually be reasonable in the circumstances. If a reasonable employer would warn an employee rather than dismiss him, or provide counselling and support rather than make him retire on health grounds, this is the benchmark by which employers will be judged. Guidelines on reasonableness are drawn from advice from government departments, codes of practice and case law established by the decisions of courts and tribunals. It is important to remember that what was considered reasonable in the past may not be considered reasonable today.

RECOGNITION OF UNIONS
See TRADE UNION.

RECRUITMENT
The process of finding and employing people to do the jobs that need to be done. It is often said that an organisation is only as good as the people it employs. It is also true that many organisations do not take as much care as they could or should in hiring people. The stages and considerations involved in the recruitment process are covered in the first essay of this book.

RED CIRCLING
A term referring to salaries that are above the maximum of a SALARY scale. This can happen following a regrading exercise or where jobs or indi-

viduals are deliberately given a premium. After a JOB EVALUATION and job grading exercise it can happen that job holders are already receiving a higher salary than the new grade rate for their jobs. The organisation may then decide to freeze the salary or give a partial increase until inflation-related and other increases have brought the salary scale to the level of what the individual is paid. Organisations that take the view that this is unfair or unpalatable may decide to create a special (personal) grade to get round the problem and enable them to give the individual concerned a salary increase.

> *Employers insist on seeing stress as an individual problem when, in reality, it's an organisational one.*
> Veronica Bayne, Civil Service Association, 1995

REDUNDANCY

Where an employer or a job ceases to exist. Euphemistically called DOWNSIZING, RIGHTSIZING or letting people go, redundancy has a specific legal definition. If employees are declared redundant but this does not comply with the legal definition, they may get higher COMPENSATION for UNFAIR DISMISSAL. For example, dismissing staff in order to employ part-timers or outsource is not redundancy because there is still a need for the work to be done.

If an organisation experiences a downturn in its business there are detailed legal rules for the notification and CONSULTATION of employees in the decision-making process, which must be transparent and reasonable. It is usually necessary for an employer to explore other options. For example, can changes be made that might prevent the redundancies? Can the number of staff potentially affected be reduced? Can any of the staff be retrained or redeployed, share the work or work part-time? Can financial or other arrangements be made to make things easier for the staff affected?

If redundancy cannot be avoided then deciding

who to make redundant must be done correctly and fairly. Organisations should have a redundancy policy stating the criteria to be applied when selecting those to be made redundant. The old maxim of LIFO (last in first out) is now seldom used. Most organisations consider employee performance, flexibility, productivity and individual wishes; for example, there may be staff willing to volunteer for redundancy. Most policies look to the future development of the organisation and to flexibility in the workforce. Employees, albeit reluctantly, now understand this.

If the criteria are not applied fairly employees may be able to claim UNFAIR DISMISSAL. Selection procedures must comply with the terms of the policy. It is acceptable to use selection tests, based on employee performance, for example, to decide on who should go. Employers are allowed considerable discretion with regard to redundancy, but they must not contravene anti-DISCRIMINATION legislation. This includes selecting part-timers or, say, homeworkers first for redundancy, where the bulk affected are female.

Compensation in the UK payable under the LAW to people made redundant is as follows.

- Half a week's pay for each year worked between the ages of 18 and 29.
- One and a half weeks' pay for each year from 41 to 65 (or whatever the normal retirement age is in an organisation).
- There is a maximum number of 20 years that can be used in the calculation, and a maximum limit of a WEEK'S PAY.

However, many organisations offer more generous terms; for example, one month's pay for every year of service. Compensation is also more generous in most parts of the European Union.

Redundancy is a complex issue that requires careful preparation and sensitive handling. Almost everyone in an organisation will be affected. For example, managers who have to make people in their department redundant are prone to STRESS, and the staff who have not been made redundant may feel insecure and demotivated.

REFERENCE

The testimony of someone regarding the character and abilities of someone else. The practice of requesting a reference is common in Australia, the UK and the USA, but not so common in the rest of Europe. Organisations that do seek references ask prospective employees to supply the name of, say, a previous employer, or, in the case of someone new to the job market, a professional person, who will supply a reference. This should not be followed up until the applicant is being considered seriously for the job, and it is good practice to inform the applicant beforehand. Applicants can then warn the relevant people if they have not already made sure that those named are willing to provide favourable references.

A reference must be true and honest. If it is not the person providing it may be sued by the employer who suffers damage as a result of relying on it, or the applicant who fails to get the job as a result of the false picture created by the reference. The UK Rehabilitation of Offenders Act 1974 states that references should not disclose spent convictions, although this is under review.

When asking for a reference the referee should be asked relevant questions and given details of the job for which the applicant is being considered. A prepaid addressed envelope may encourage a prompt response. It is sensible to obtain a reference before offering someone a job or to make a job offer conditional on receiving satisfactory references. However, no one is obliged to provide a reference, and some organisations will not supply one where a conditional offer has been made in case they are held responsible for any subsequent withdrawal of the offer. Some organisations provide only standard letters to ex-employees whose performance has been satisfactory; some will answer only specific questions put to them. Other organisations provide the employee with an "open" reference, often commencing with the rubric "To whom this may concern". Alternatively, organisations may only give a reference by telephone; others may be willing to provide additional information by telephone.

The more senior the post, the more important it is for employers to get references, and it is often the case that people will say more on the telephone than they are prepared to put in a letter. A sensible precaution with all references is to ask two questions.

1 Is there anything unusual about the people the applicant has given, or perhaps omitted to give, as referees?
2 What, if anything, can be read between the lines of the reference provided?

RELIGION

Practical as well as legal problems can arise if employees of particular religions are not recruited, promoted or, perhaps, not allowed to attend important religious festivals. In the UK (apart from Northern Ireland) there is no legislation on religious DISCRIMINATION. Some groups (such as Jews), however, are classified as ethnic groups as well as religious groups. Refusal to give people time off for religious festivals and so on should usually be avoided, although it is reasonable to require that the time is made up through working extra hours on other days.

REMUNERATION

Defined by the *Oxford English Dictionary* as "... reward, pay for service rendered... what is received as pay", remuneration may include BENEFITS such as PENSIONS. Management should develop a remuneration policy that helps with the RECRUITMENT, retention and motivation of employees.

REPETITIVE STRAIN INJURY

A physical condition that, among other things, has been attributed to using keyboards, the symptoms of which include pain or numbness, generally in the hands, wrists, elbows and arms. Although it was for a long time not taken seriously by many employers, judges and even some doctors, repetitive strain injury (RSI) is increasingly recognised as a genuine complaint throughout western industrial society. In the UK and in many European countries, especially Germany and the Nordic countries, RSI and other musculo-skeletal disorders have been targeted by the Health and Safety Executive (HSE) as a major element in lost working days, totalling around 5.5m each year and costing some £1 billion in SICK PAY. (See *A Pain in your Workplace?*, an HSE publication.) The consensus of advice is to seek treatment as soon as the signs appear and to change working patterns. The cause of the condition is not certain but incorrect posture at any type of workstation is likely to be a major factor. When working with a keyboard, the elbow should be in the same horizontal plane as the middle row of the keyboard. (See also DISPLAY SCREEN EQUIPMENT.)

REPRESENTATIONAL RIGHTS OF UNIONS
See TRADE UNION.

Differences of opinion should be valued, not counter attacked.
Mary Parker Follett

REPRESENTATIVES
People who represent employees to management. LAW increasingly requires all organisations, not just those with unions, to formalise their arrangements, especially for HEALTH AND SAFETY. Representatives can be elected by employees or by other means.

As well as representation for health and safety and, if applicable, on works councils, employees are usually entitled to have someone to represent their interests in disciplinary matters. In this case the employee chooses the representative.

Rights to employee representatives, whether or not unions are present, are becoming common throughout the European Union. All employees should be prepared to develop formal and appropriate structures to facilitate them. If representatives suffer a DETRIMENT in performing this role they can complain to an INDUSTRIAL TRIBUNAL.

RESIGNATION

The communication of a decision by an employee to quit, which is sometimes made in haste and later regretted. An organisation's STAFF HANDBOOK should state that any resignation must be in writing. It is equally important that any resignation is accepted in writing; verbal resignations can be disputed. (See NOTICE; TERMINATION OF EMPLOYMENT.)

REST AND WELFARE FACILITIES

Most employers provide their employees with some rest and welfare facilities, even if it is only a cloakroom or a drinks vending machine. What an organisation provides depends on its size, its CULTURE and the nature of the work. Good facilities are appreciated by job applicants and current employees, who see them as perks and a measure of how much their employer values them. Some facilities must be provided by law under, for example, the Workplace Regulations 1992. These relate especially to hygiene, but there are also special provisions covering disabled people and pregnant women.

RESTRAINT OF TRADE CLAUSE

A device to prevent (or reduce the ability of) employees who leave to set up their own business by poaching customers and clients. Many employers include a clause in the CONTRACT OF EMPLOYMENT for certain staff preventing them from working in a competing business within a given area for a period of time. However, a balance must be struck as the LAW also needs to protect the ex-employee's right to work, so the restraint has to be reasonable. This depends on the type of business and the skill or rarity value of the employee. A marketing manager, a research chemist or an investment analyst, for example, will potentially be able to inflict more damage than, say, a highly skilled mechanic, a teacher or a cook. Professional advice should be sought on drafting such clauses.

RETIREMENT

When someone finally stops working, although there are many people who continue to work in some way after they have retired. The age at which people must (or normally do) retire from an organisation should be stated in the CONTRACT OF EMPLOYMENT. In the UK it is usually between 55 and 65 but some people, such as judges, do not have to retire until they are 70. The state retirement age, when people become eligible for a state retirement pension, is 65 for men and 60 for women. The state retirement age for women will rise in stages to 65 between 2010 and 2020. It is unlawful to insist that a woman retires at a different age from a man. Early retirement may be agreed between employer and an employee, for example, if an employee suffers from an ILLNESS or an employer wants to replace someone who has not reached retirement age. Compulsory retirement before contractual retirement age can result in a successful claim for UNFAIR DISMISSAL.

Ex-gratia payments to people when they retire are an unapproved pension benefit and are fully taxable. Lump-sum payments from an approved pension scheme are tax free. Rulings by the EUROPEAN COURT OF JUSTICE have established that PAY under the EQUAL PAY article of the Treaty of Rome also includes PENSIONS and, through the calculation of pensions, retirement ages. Pressures to equalise retirement ages under occupational schemes on these grounds, combined with financial pressures on state systems as a result of demographic forces, have lead to a gradual raising of retirement ages in Europe. This has taken the form of either a progressive raising of women's retirement age with a withdrawal of early retirement options or the introduction of phased retirement for men and women over a common age range, with reductions in pensions for early retirement and enhanced pensions for those who work longer. In Germany a scheme allows for retirement on half previous hours at 70% of pay. In France staged retirement is possible between the ages of 55 and 65, with full early retirement on a pension at age 58 provided a young person is employed to fill the vacancy.

RIGHTSIZING

When the term DOWNSIZING, with its connotation of large-scale job losses, started to go out of fashion in the late 1980s, people started to talk about rightsizing. The implication is that to maintain strategic advantage and long-term competitiveness, a business has to be the right size, that is, it should employ the appropriate number of staff. The following US definition of rightsizing will appeal to those who enjoy 52 words where ten will normally suffice: "an integrated, internally consistent and externally legitimate configuration of organisational processes, products and people based on a shared VISION of the future of the organisation and a clearly articulated mission and a strategy supported by management, well understood by members of the organisation, and in which members have a sense of ownership".

> *Why don't we stop re-engineering, delayering, restructuring, centralising and decentralising and instead start thinking.*
> Henry Mintzberg

ROLE DESCRIPTION

The part to be played by employees in meeting the objectives of their jobs. It covers the behavioural aspects of the job rather than the finite tasks that the job involves. (See JOB DESCRIPTION.)

RSI

See REPETITIVE STRAIN INJURY.

RUDENESS

Something that exists mainly in the eyes and ears of the offended. The degree to which language, gestures or other behaviour are considered rude depends largely on an individual's background. Initially, all employees can do is make it clear when they think someone (lower, higher, or equal in the hierarchy) has been rude to them. Persistent rudeness may amount to HARASSMENT, which can be dealt with formally through an organisation's GRIEVANCE PROCEDURE. Employees who are rude to outsiders, such as potential customers, are bad for business. It is therefore important that anyone whose job involves outside contacts is chosen carefully and given the appropriate training.

SALARY

A synonym for WAGES, salary has traditionally been the word to describe the monthly income of white-collar administrative and managerial employees. A salary may be categorised into "basic salary" and "total salary", which contains more than one component, for example, a bonus payment. Salaries may be described as PAY or compensation.

SCIENTIFIC MANAGEMENT

Many of the profound changes that have taken place in manufacturing industry are the result of Frederick Winslow Taylor's system of scientific management. He is berated today as the "carrot and stick" man. Carrot yes, stick no. Taylor, who had been a lathe operator and a supervisor, saw the main flaw in the old methods of manufacturing: that there was no method. He knew that he could help increase the low earnings of the workers and increase profits.

Taylor was the first person to study and measure work. He divided manufacturing into its component parts and showed that if individuals were highly trained in their tasks, merely by using better techniques they could double their output. Taylor changed not only work but also the nature of management. He separated the roles of worker and management, implementing production planning and control where none had existed before.

Taylor's colleague, Henry Gantt, designed the new pay system for scientific management. The old piece-work rates were abolished. Every task had a written procedure on how to do it and how long it should take. Gantt's pay system was a day rate based on what management considered was the minimum acceptable output from a worker, plus a bonus for every item produced above that number. It was greeted with cries of "they'll take advantage of us" from the employees. The foremen also got a bonus for each worker that achieved his target, plus an extra bonus if every worker in the TEAM hit the target. The role of foreman was defined as "training the workers so that they can achieve target".

As general manager of the Bethlehem steel works, Taylor spent 30 years developing the system, which has been used by just about every factory in this century. In his time he was considered a liberal and disliked by both company owners and the unions. Scientific management was a dramatic change to the structure of the workplace and, inevitably, society. As with most management tools, it was seldom applied precisely as the creator intended. With scientific management, managers got hooked on the big stick of measurement, and fooling the TIME AND MOTION man became the most widespread game in industry.

SEARCHING EMPLOYEES

If the nature of a business suggests that there may be occasions when an employer wishes to search employees, their belongings, lockers, bags, desks and vehicles at or when leaving the workplace, a contractual right to do so must be established by including a statement in the company rules referred to in the CONTRACT OF EMPLOYMENT or STAFF HANDBOOK. If there is no clause but an employer has reasonable suspicions that, say, THEFT has occurred, it is possible to make a citizen's arrest as long as the employee is told what it is about and the police are called. In this way the employee can be detained. It is best to leave the searching to the police.

SECONDARY ACTION

See INDUSTRIAL ACTION.

SECONDMENT

Where an employee remains employed by one organisation but is seconded to work for another organisation. Secondment occurs for many different reasons, including to support initiatives such as Business in the Community, to gain work experience or to provide advice and support to organisations. For example, journalists working for *The Economist* are sometimes seconded to the World Bank. Throughout a secondment individuals remain the responsibility of the original employer with regard to the DUTY OF CARE and the terms of their CONTRACT OF EMPLOYMENT. In practice, however, the organisation to which they are seconded may indemnify the original employer in respect of claims for which it is at fault.

SELF-DIRECTED TEAM

A formal and permanent group whose members work together full-time, as opposed to occasional and transient groups such as project teams or quality circles. Self-directed team members are multiskilled and aim to be able to do most or all of the team's tasks. They are trained and empowered, and they accept responsibility for some or all of the management tasks that would previously have been done by their immediate manager. Which management tasks and how much responsibility is devolved depends on the management skills available within the team, the acceptance of responsibilities by the team, and the outcome of weighing potential performance improvements against risk.

SELF-EMPLOYED

When someone works on their own account and is not an employee (see EMPLOYMENT STATUS). Self-employed people have no right to a period of NOTICE, unless they negotiate it, they cannot claim for REDUNDANCY or UNFAIR DISMISSAL and, generally, they will not be paid when sick or on holiday. They are, however, protected against racial and SEXUAL DISCRIMINATION. They are responsible for their own income tax arrangements and do not have tax deducted through the PAYE scheme.

SENIORITY

A term that refers to an employee's position in the hierarchy or length of service in an organisation. Many organisations, recognising that the commitment shown and the experience gained by long-standing employees are valuable assets, reward such individuals by giving them, say, a GIFT, a framed certificate or an increase in paid HOLIDAY.

Central and local government in the UK and continental Europe have a system of automatic annual pay increases within each hierarchical grade. These pay structures, commonly called step pay structures, offer an increase in pay every 12 months until you reach the top of the scale for that grade regardless of your performance.

This system is also found in private companies in continental Europe. In the UK and the USA private industry mostly operates on a rate for the job, which is related to both external market and internal relativities. In most Japanese companies seniority in the company hierarchy is dependent solely upon length of service and age.

SERPS
State Earnings Related Pension Scheme (see PENSIONS).

We are what we repeatedly do. Excellence, then, is not an act but a habit.
Aristotle

SEVEN Ss
The system devised by the McKinsey team of Richard Pascale, Tom Peters and Richard Waterman to measure the quality of a company's performance. The seven factors are divided into three hard:

- strategy
- structure
- systems

and four soft:

- style
- shared values
- skills
- staff

Pascale used the model when comparing Japanese companies in his book, *The Art of*

Japanese Management, and Peters and Waterman used it in their book, *In Search of Excellence*.

SEXUAL DISCRIMINATION

DISCRIMINATION against people because of their sex. Legislation outlawing sexual discrimination has been introduced in many countries to promote EQUAL OPPORTUNITY for men and women. In the UK the Sex Discrimination Acts 1975 and 1986 prohibit sexual discrimination in respect of advertising and selection for appointment, promotion, transfer, training and DISMISSAL, and the Equal Pay Act 1970 makes it illegal to pay people of different sexes different rates for the same or an equivalent job (see EQUAL PAY). The LAW protects employees who suffer VICTIMISATION for exercising or attempting to exercise their rights under the acts.

It is equally unlawful for an employee to discriminate against a colleague on the ground of sex. All staff must co-operate with an organisation's measures to ensure equal opportunities and non-discrimination. A complaint of unlawful discrimination in the workplace must be made to an INDUSTRIAL TRIBUNAL within three months of the date of the perceived discrimination. The UK acts are supported by Codes of Practice prepared by the Equal Opportunities Commission (EOC) and the Commission for Racial Equality (CRE) and approved by Parliament. The acts do not apply to firms with five or fewer employees.

SEXUAL ORIENTATION

The Sex Discrimination Act applies to both men and women. It defines DISCRIMINATION in relation to gender and can now extend to acts of discrimination on grounds of sexual orientation, the avoidance of which is best dealt with in the company's policy on HARASSMENT and BULLYING. (See DIGNITY AT WORK.)

SHIFT WORK

An arrangement used by businesses that need to operate for longer than standard hours per day or week. In the case of 24-hour operations employees are often organised to work in shifts, say, 6am–2pm, 2pm–10pm and 10pm–6am. A variety of other working arrangements can be put in place depending on the demands. The new customer service and telephone help desk operations commonly have staff working just three 11-hour shifts in each week. Shift work can give rise to STRESS (see NIGHT WORK). Shift work is widespread in the USA and Europe but less common in Scandinavian countries.

SICK PAY

People who are off work because they are sick still need money to live on. In the UK employers are responsible for paying Statutory Sick Pay (SSP) for up to 28 weeks to employees who are incapable of working under their CONTRACT OF EMPLOYMENT because of ILLNESS or disablement. This money is only partially reimbursed by the government provided certain conditions are met and on the understanding that employers exercise reasonable control over sickness ABSENCE qualifying for SSP. Since April 6th 1994 women over the age of 60 have been entitled to SSP. Employees are not entitled to SSP if they:

- are pensioners;
- have a contract of three months or less;
- have average weekly earnings below the LOWER EARNINGS LIMIT, the point at which NATIONAL INSURANCE contributions become payable;
- were entitled to invalidity benefit, severe disablement allowance or maternity pay in the previous eight weeks;
- have done no work under their contract of employment;
- are involved in a trade dispute, unless they were sick before the dispute began, or are able to prove that they are not participating or interested in the dispute;
- are pregnant;
- are abroad outside the European Union on the first day of the period of incapacity for

work (PIW);
- are in legal custody;
- have just joined the company and were in receipt of SSP from their former employer, and there is a gap of eight weeks or more between the two PIWs.

The legislation is contained in the Social Security Contributions and Benefits Act 1992, the Social Security Administration Act 1992 and the Statutory Sick Pay Act 1994. Employers must keep detailed records of SSP. If an employee's absence through sickness continues after 28 weeks, the responsibility for paying SSP transfers to the Department of Social Security (DSS).

Entitlement to SSP begins on the fourth qualifying day of absence because of incapacity to work. The PIW is any four or more consecutive days of incapacity, including Sundays and holidays, regardless of whether the employee would normally have worked on those days. It is up to an employer to determine when an employee must give notification of sick absence, and the employer must ensure that all employees are aware of these requirements.

Employers are free to draw up their own rules on reporting and producing evidence of illness. However, an employer cannot demand a doctor's certificate before the end of seven calendar days of illness. Statutory or company sick pay may be withheld if the employee fails to follow the proper procedures. If SSP is not paid and the employee disagrees, the employer must give written reasons to the employee, who may appeal to the DSS for a decision.

Many companies run their own sick pay schemes that are more generous than the statutory one, often maintaining full pay for several weeks and even continuing some payments beyond the legally required 28 weeks. These extended payments are usually covered by the company taking out what is usually known as private health insurance (PHI) or long-term disability insurance. This is not the same as private medical insurance.

SMOKING AT WORK

More and more businesses throughout Europe and in most of the developed world are introducing policies that restrict or ban smoking in the workplace. In part this reflects changing social attitudes towards smoking, but firms are also taking action in order to conform with HEALTH AND SAFETY legislation and to avoid the threat of litigation from non-smoking employees claiming they have become ill as a result of passive smoking at work. In the UK, for example, legislation has existed for many years outlawing smoking in such occupations as catering and food production, but since 1992, under the Management of Health and Safety at Work Regulations, companies have had to assess and respond to all workplace risks to health and safety. Furthermore, under the Health Safety and Welfare Regulations 1992, employers must provide rest facilities for non-smokers, but they are not obliged to make provision for smokers. This means that if canteens, lounges and other social areas cannot be divided in a way that prevents smoke drifting into non-smoking sections, they must be subject to a no-smoking rule.

Introducing a no-smoking policy must be done lawfully, which normally means that all existing employees should be consulted, and employees who will have difficulty in complying should be identified and given time to adjust to the change. Ideally, help should also be offered to those who want to stop smoking. The CONTRACT OF EMPLOYMENT for new staff should explain the policy on smoking and the DISCIPLINARY PROCEDURE that applies to those who fail to comply. There are other considerations. A total ban may result in visitors to an organisation's PREMISES having to walk through a huddle of smokers gathered around the entrance and a heap of cigarette butts on the ground. Or it may result in employees going off to smoke in obscure parts of the building where they may cause a fire risk. Even if smoking is allowed in designated places at designated times, non-smokers may complain that they are putting in more hours of work than smokers.

Smoking continues to be more widespread and socially acceptable in continental Europe than in the UK, with the density of smoke increasing the nearer you get to the Mediterranean. In Germany employers must make provisions for non-smokers but are forbidden by the constitution to ban smoking entirely on their premises. In France a law regulating smoking at the workplace was introduced in 1993, although it merely prescribes what common sense would suggest.

SOCIAL CHAPTER

The UK term for the Agreement on Social Policy added as a separate item to the Maastricht treaty and enforced via the Protocol on Social Policy, which allowed the UK to opt out of its provisions. The Social Chapter – not to be confused with the SOCIAL CHARTER – introduced a number of changes to the procedures for arriving at EU legislation in the employment and social fields. Specifically, it allowed more subjects to be introduced via qualified majority vote of national ministers on the Council of Ministers and also created scope for the SOCIAL PARTNERS at European level to have more opportunity to examine the European Commission's legislative proposals and, if they wish, to conclude an agreement to regulate an issue. The effect of the UK opt-out was to clear the way for the other member states to agree a directive on European works councils which the UK had previously blocked. The social partners also came to an agreement on PARENTAL LEAVE in 1996.

The ending of the opt-out by the Labour government means that the UK will become subject to these measures, and will also participate in the framing of any future social policy initiatives which pass through the successor mechanisms to the Social Chapter agreed at the 1997 Intergovernmental Conference.

SOCIAL CHARTER

The Social Charter (Community Charter of the Fundamental Social Rights of Workers) was adopted not as legislation but in the form of a solemn declaration in 1989 by all the then member states of the European Community with the exception of the UK. It set out a list of principles for a social dimension of basic standards to apply in all countries. These were to accompany and mitigate the effects of the single market, subsequently concretised as the Social Charter Action Programme, which proposed all the recent directives in the social and employment sphere. In particular, the proposals that flowed from the Social Charter were intended to allay the fears of employees and their trade unions in northern Europe that the development of the single market could endanger their employment standards by allowing companies to move production to, and import from, countries with lower standards in a process dubbed social dumping. The 1989 Social Charter should not be confused with the SOCIAL CHAPTER, nor with the 1961 European Social Charter of the Council of Europe.

SOCIAL PARTNERS

Euro-speak for trade unions and employers' organisations. Ideas for legislation at EU level are increasingly developed and debated via the "social dialogue" between the main organisations for each side: the European Trade Union Confederation (ETUC), Union des confédérations de l'industrie et des employeurs d'Europe (UNICE – private-sector employers) and Centre européen des entreprises publiques (CEEP – public-sector employers).

STAFF HANDBOOK

In the UK and the USA there is some information which by LAW must appear in the written STATEMENT OF TERMS OF WORK. Other information is more conveniently put into a staff handbook, which may form part of the CONTRACT OF EMPLOYMENT. This can be used to inform employees about all aspects of their employment and the company, its policies and procedures. It can include a welcome message from the CEO and statements about the company's VISION, MISSION and values. It can even include information about facilities in the locality. A loose-leaf binder sensibly allows for changes and insertions.

STATEMENT OF TERMS OF WORK

Most legal systems require all employees to have written confirmation of their basic terms of work. It must be given to those who are employed for one month or more within two months of the start date. Most organisations supply such statements before the employment begins. A statement of terms of work is not a legally binding contract unless the employer wishes it to be or it can be interpreted as one. It should be seen as part of an organisation's internal communication system, so care should be taken in its presentation, readability and accuracy. Employees rightly attach importance to these documents and can pick up a hidden agenda if the document is aggressive or offhand. A letter is sufficient as long as it contains the following information:

- when the work started;
- whether previous employment will count for CONTINUITY of employment purposes;
- PLACE OF WORK;
- HOURS OF WORK;
- PAY and the method of calculation;
- JOB TITLE;
- period of NOTICE;
- how terms of work are arrived at (for example, from collective agreement).

Standard form documents are available from law stationers and there are many guides on how to write a statement. It is important, however, that the document reflects the needs and priorities of the employer. Employees can be referred by the principal document to other documents such as a STAFF HANDBOOK for arrangements for SICK PAY, PENSIONS, DISCIPLINARY PROCEDURE, GRIEVANCE PROCEDURE.

STRESS

An old word, probably derived from distress,

commonly used in the workplace to imply a human condition brought about by pressure felt by someone to achieve or conform. Some people find the world more stressful to deal with than others. Anxiety and worry can build up in certain people and result in depression and even apparently unrelated physical ILLNESS. Others who are subject to unrelenting and unreasonable pressure may simply, as a means of self-preservation, switch off and stop caring about their performance.

The causes of stress are well understood and most stress in preventable. One of the main causes is worry about the future, so freeing the mind of "what if" thoughts can make a huge difference in relieving stress. Effective time management is also helpful: avoid knee-jerk reactions; stand back from an awkward situation and count to ten; take a lunch break; and do not work excessively long hours. The worst remedy is to resort to drink. ALCOHOL is a depressant, so if you are feeling low it will push you further down.

Failure to minimise the risk of stress can breach the Health and Safety at Work Regulations 1992, and has given rise to successful claims of negligence. Employers can do a lot to reduce the potential for stress in their workforce, starting with effective and continuous communication and a climate that encourages good internal relationships. Research has produced a long list of stress builders:

- lack of security, opportunities, interest, feedback, clarity of role, support, praise and recognition, authority, ability to control own environment and ability to influence;
- the effects of change or perceived change;
- a heavy workload;
- a skills mismatch and lack of training leading to lack of confidence;
- an aggressive or bullying boss.

There are, however, levels of stress that our minds accept as motivators. A challenge may be stressful to start with, but the pressure – not too

> *Anxiety is like sand in an oyster; a few grains produce a pearl, too many kill.*
> Old Chinese proverb

STRIKE
See INDUSTRIAL ACTION.

SSP
Statutory SICK PAY.

SUBCONTRACTING
See OUTSOURCING.

SUBSIDIARITY
The principle of subsidiarity, as enunciated by Pope Leo X in 1947, is that "it is an injustice, a grave evil and a disturbance of right order for a large and higher organisation to arrogate itself functions which can be performed efficiently by smaller and lower bodies". This is a clear statement for participation and against bureaucracy from an organisation perceived by many to be a rigid bureaucracy.

SUNDAY WORK
This is a controversial matter. In some EU countries it remains rare, but it is a growing phenomenon in, for example, Germany and the Netherlands. In the UK it is fairly widespread, but under the Employment Rights Act 1996 employees are allowed to opt out of Sunday work.

SUSPENSION FROM WORK
There are two circumstances that may lead to suspension from work.

1 Suspension with or without pay as part of a DISCIPLINARY PROCEDURE. This should be catered for in the published disciplinary rules and procedures, otherwise suspension without pay amounts to

BREACH OF CONTRACT by the employer.

2 Suspension because it would endanger an employee's health were he or she to continue working, for example, when pregnant.

T

TEAM

This is a fashionable word, although NETWORK is fast taking over. We often use the word team to mean the whole company, because unless everyone pulls together we will not achieve our goals. But it is difficult to weld, motivate, coach and manage more than dozen people into a close-knit team. A team is best defined as a small number of people with complementary skills who are committed to a common purpose, performance goals and approach, for which they hold themselves mutually accountable. A company may be made up of many small teams, all working in harmony. This alone is a challenge, since our culture promotes inter-team rivalry. For a company the answer lies in the allocation of the responsibility and accountability for decision-making.

TEAM BRIEFINGS

A two-way communication system, although the impetus for holding the briefings comes from the top. The primary purpose is to communicate corporate policies, financial progress and other information that staff need to be aware of. Team briefings underline the basis of a manager's role: to inform the staff. It is a cascading system, whereby the top team brief their subordinates and so on down the organisation, with everybody giving exactly the same information. To achieve their purpose, team briefings should be regular, with question and answer time to allow feedback. This is the aspect that takes time to evolve. Staff need to feel that there is complete trust, and that comments will be paid genuine attention to, before they will speak up.

TEAM BUILDING

Together Everyone Achieves More = TEAM. This slogan has yet to be bettered as a simple definition of why companies are promoting TEAM WORK. Effective teams do not just happen. They are built, like champion sports teams. Team members need to understand and trust each other. They need a clear idea of what they are expected to achieve as a team. They need a coach who can identify their strengths, their latent talents, and the areas where they need to strengthen their abilities. Research has indicated that for a team to be effective, its members must:

- understand personal and team goals;
- not seek personal gain at the expense of other team members;
- recognise their interdependence;
- recognise the benefits of collaboration;
- feel a sense of team ownership;
- practise open and honest communication within the team;
- work in a climate of trust;
- express openly ideas, opinions and feelings;
- listen when others speak;
- make an effort to understand each other's points of view;
- recognise that differences of opinion are inevitable, and work together to resolve conflict quickly and constructively;
- receive the support of all other team members;
- enjoy working together;
- have fun.

TEAM WORK

Regardless of the nature of the team, its tasks or its reason for existing, working together productively and without recrimination is the most difficult element for most team members. Considerable research carried out at Henley Management College in the UK by Meredith Belbin has produced a clear picture of the types of people needed to ensure effective team work. Belbin lists eight types and gives them role labels.

1 Co-ordinator. Mature, confident, clarifies goals, promotes decision making, delegates well.
2 Shaper. Challenging, dynamic, thrives on pressure. Has the drive to overcome obstacles.
3 Plant. Creative imaginative, unorthodox. Solves difficult problems.

4 Resource investigator. Extrovert, enthusiastic, communicative, networker, explores opportunities.

5 Implementer. Disciplined, reliable, efficient. Turns ideas into practical actions.

6 Monitor/evaluator. Strategic, discerning, sober. Sees all options, judges accurately.

7 Completer/finisher. Painstaking, conscientious, anxious. Searches out errors, delivers on time.

8 Team worker. Cooperative, mild, perceptive, diplomatic. Listens, averts friction, calms.

Belbin states that all roles must be present in an effective team, so if a team has fewer than eight members some must double up their roles. If a team has more than eight members it is easy to see where to have several members with the same role. However, Belbin warns against having more than one plant; they will fight against each other's ideas.

TECs
See TRAINING AND ENTERPRISE COUNCILS.

TEMPORARY WORK
See AGENCY STAFF; CASUAL WORKER; FIXED-TERM CONTRACT.

TERMINATION OF EMPLOYMENT
On the employer's part, firing someone or making them redundant. On the employee's part, resigning. How a CONTRACT OF EMPLOYMENT is ended should be made clear; for example, what is the length of NOTICE, what entitles the employer to dismiss someone instantly (see DISMISSAL).

THEFT
Criminal behaviour is rife in the workplace. Many employees routinely take items of company property to use at home. Research has revealed that most employees, even the most senior staff, regard the theft of stationery items and suchlike as acceptable pilfering. Many organisations accept

this in the same way as they may turn a blind eye to people making personal telephone calls during working hours. But every organisation needs to draw the line somewhere and to make clear in its rules of conduct what its attitude is to theft and what disciplinary measures it will take. Instances of stealing from other employees should be treated seriously, as a spate of thefts can result in a damaging lack of trust between employees.

THEORIES X AND Y

Theory X (authoritarian management) assumes that most people are lazy, dislike work and need some carrot and stick to perform; and that they are basically immature, need direction and are incapable of taking responsibility. Plato said: "Authoritarian direction is needed if anything of value is to be achieved."

Theory Y (participative management) assumes the opposite, that people have a psychological need to do something worthwhile, and seek responsibility and achievement; that they are in fact adult. They act as children only when bullied by Theory X managers. Aristotle said: "Man is a social animal who seeks a sense of participation in his own destiny."

These theories were articulated by Douglas McGregor of MIT in 1960. McGregor also expanded on Abraham Maslow's HIERARCHY OF NEEDS by adding the need for continuing self-development to the top of the pyramid. Maslow chastised McGregor for belittling people in Theory X, but he liked Theory Y and set out to test it. The results, even in a company wholeheartedly committed to the concept, were not wholly successful. Maslow concluded that Theory Y was not the whole answer and suggested there was a need for a Theory Z. This was subsequently explored by William Ouchi in his book *Theory Z: The Japanese Challenge*.

THERBLIG

Lilian and Frank Gilbreth took F.W. Taylor's idea of SCIENTIFIC MANAGEMENT and developed their own powerful measuring system for the study of TIME AND MOTION, in which therbligs were the symbols used to identify the many motions used in completing a task.

THIRTEENTH MONTH SALARY

Most employees in continental Europe receive extra pay over and above their 12-monthly salaries. This is dubbed the 13th month salary, although in most cases it is not paid out in one lump but is divided into a Christmas bonus and a summer bonus. It may or may not be exactly equal to one month's pay, depending on the country and local CUSTOM AND PRACTICE. Where they can, employers are trying to tie the payment to meeting conditions, such as good attendance. In Spain employees also receive a 14th or even a 15th month salary.

TIME AND MOTION STUDY

A way of formally measuring work. Men would be employed to go round a factory, observe what the employees did and time how long they took to do it. The results would then be analysed to determine whether the task each worker was responsible for could be done more efficiently. (See SCIENTIFIC MANAGEMENT; THERBLIG.)

TIME LIMITS

If a CONTRACT OF EMPLOYMENT is ended, albeit unlawfully, how much time does the "victim" have to take legal action? The answer is, generally not a lot. Most complaints to an INDUSTRIAL TRIBUNAL must be made within three months of the incident (for example, DISMISSAL); for REDUNDANCY it is six months. If, however, the claim is for BREACH OF CONTRACT in the courts it is six years; for NEGLIGENCE it is three years. All jurisdictions have some time limits. If you are out of time, even by one day, you are out of the running.

TIME OFF

An employee has no legal right to take time off for personal reasons, but in practice employers often allow employees to go to the dentist or doctor during working hours. They may encourage them to do this first thing in the morning or late in the day to minimise the disruption the ABSENCE may cause. The amount of time off work employees are allowed to take may depend on their length of service and the reason for the LEAVE. The main reasons and UK statutory requirements are listed below.

Antenatal care Pregnant employees must be allowed time off to go to antenatal clinics provided they:

- have an appointment and have asked their employer for the time off;
- if requested by the employer, produce a certificate stating that they are pregnant and an appointment card indicating the time and the date of the appointment.

Public duty Employers are required to give employees reasonable time off to perform certain duties, such as being a member of a local authority or a National Health Service trust, or a school governor or prison visitor. There is no statutory right to be paid for time off for these activities, but there are statutory criteria for determining what is reasonable time off for public duties. These are:

- the amount of time off needed to carry out the duties and the amount of time off the employee has already had in respect of them;
- the circumstances of the employer's business and the effect the employee's absence will have on the running of the business.

Redundancy Employees who have received notice of DISMISSAL for redundancy and have at least two years' service are entitled during their periods of notice to reasonable time off with pay to look for other employment, or to arrange for training for future employment.

Safety REPRESENTATIVES Safety representatives are entitled to take time off with pay in circumstances covered by the Safety Representatives and Safety Committee's Regulations 1977 and the Health and Safety at Work Act 1974.

TRADE UNION duties and activities An employee who is a member of a recognised trade union is allowed to take reasonable time off to take part in any trade union activity, such as voting in union elections. Employees who are officials of a recognised trade union are also allowed reasonable time off to carry out certain trade union duties, such as negotiations with the employer on matters specified by legislation.

TIP

A payment made to an individual by a person who has received a service supplied by the individual. Tips are not part of the individual's wages, but they are taxable. The way organisations deal with the payment of tips to individuals varies around the world and between businesses. For example, some restaurants have compulsory service charges so the owners have to decide whether the basic wage will include an allowance for the service charge. They should inform individuals working for them (who may or may not be employees) how the payment system works. (See also GIFT.)

TRADE DISPUTE

Defined by the Trade Union and Labour Relations (Consolidation) Act 1992 as: "A dispute between employers and workers, or between workers and workers which is connected with one or more of the following:

- terms and conditions of employment;
- physical working conditions;
- termination or suspension or engagement or non-engagement of an individual;
- suspension of employment duties;
- allocation of work;
- discipline issues;
- membership or non-membership of a TRADE UNION;
- facilities for trade union officials;
- negotiation or CONSULTATION process or procedure."

It is usual for organisations to have a dispute procedure with an agreed framework to resolve collective disputes and individual grievances. In the UK the procedure must be negotiated with the trade unions concerned, if they are recognised. The procedure can include reference to external mediation, conciliation or ARBITRATION (see ACAS). Some industries have industry-wide disputes procedures. If a dispute occurs that involves INDUSTRIAL ACTION such as a strike, the trade union will be immune only if the dispute is between "workers and their employer".

TRADE UNION

An association of employees who have common interests based on their occupation or employment. A trade union's role is to protect and advance its members' interests as employees, particularly in respect of terms and conditions of employment. Trade unions are also concerned with improving the skills of their members.

A trade union usually has to submit a claim for recognition to an employer. The employer then decides whether or not to recognise the union. If the employer believes that COLLECTIVE BARGAINING on the terms and conditions of employment would be to the organisation's advantage, recognition of a union or staff association for that purpose can take place. The way negotiations are carried out will be determined by a procedure agreement. If more than one union seeks recognition the employer can opt for single-union or multi-union recognition. Employers prefer single-union recognition agreements because they are more straightforward to operate and they can give the organisation an advantage over competitors that have multi-union recognition agreements.

At local level, union members are usually represented by shop stewards who are employees of the same organisation as the union members. Full-time union officials are usually called in only when management and trade unions cannot reach agreement. The representational rights of a union will depend on whether or not it is recognised for negotiation purposes.

Trade union membership varies considerably within the European Union, from below 10% of the workforce in France to over 70% in Scandinavia. The UK, Germany and Italy are in the mid-range with 30–35% of their workforces in trade unions, and they are all on a declining trend. This is most marked in the UK where trade union membership has fallen from a peak of 50% of the workforce in 1979. After falling for several years, trade union membership is rising in the Netherlands; this may be an indication that trade union decline is not the inevitable trend suggested by some observers. Why trade union membership varies among countries is a complex issue. Some crucial factors are the role of unions in providing key social benefits, such as unemployment pay, for their members; support for trade unionism from legislation; the political complexion of trade unions and an absence of cut-throat competition between different politically inspired confederations; and a willingness by employers to recognise unions for bargaining purposes. Irrespective of national differences in the EU, most European companies with more than 200 employees recognise trade unions.

The election of the Conservative Party under Margaret Thatcher in the UK marked the beginning of a substantial decline of union influence as legislation was introduced to curb union power and ban the CLOSED SHOP, and the unions ceased to have the cosy consultative relationship they had enjoyed under the previous Labour government. Most trade unions in the UK are affiliated to the Trades Union Congress (TUC), which co-ordinates trade union activities, provides advice to its members and mediates in the case of internal disputes. It has, however, no authority over individual unions. The Commissioner for Protection Against Unlawful Industrial Action is concerned with applications from parties for assistance in proceedings against unions or individuals resulting from unlawful industrial action. The Commissioner for the Rights of Trade Union Members provides assistance to individuals who may wish to institute proceedings against their union, or an official or trustee of the union.

> *The mainstay of training is confidence. That's why we show them how to let a tank run over them. It gets their confidence up.*
> Officer in charge of US special operations command

TRAINEE
A trainee may be found in any area of work and can be any age. Training arrangements may be formal or informal. For example, various government and company schemes provide a formal framework for the training of individuals (see APPRENTICESHIP). Employers may be able to apply for training grants if they take part in a government scheme. Trainees involved in government-sponsored training schemes are not employees as they have no CONTRACT OF EMPLOYMENT with the organisation providing the training. If the trainee is a YOUNG WORKER then certain legal constraints may apply.

TRAINING AND ENTERPRISE COUNCILS
An initiative set up and funded by the UK government and the EU to help and advise UK business. There are Training and Enterprise Councils (TECs) throughout the UK (they are called Local Enterprise Councils or LECs in Scotland), with boards of directors drawn from public and private industry. Their most recent initiative was the setting up of advice and consultancy services called BUSINESS LINKS.

TRANSACTIONAL ANALYSIS
A transaction is the basic unit of behaviour. A says or does something to B and B says or does something to A. Transactional analysis (TA) was invented by a psychiatrist, Eric Berne, to interpret personality problems. However, he soon realised that it could be more widely used to achieve better communication. The symbols of TA are three

circles that represent the three parts of an individual's personality: parent, adult, child. TA determines which of the three elements is used to initiate a transaction and from which element the response comes. If initiation and response are from the same element, the result is understanding and acceptance; if the transaction is crossed, the result is misunderstanding and problems.

Berne proved by physical experiment that our brains are a kind of tape recorder of everything that has happened to us. In our first five formative years we make a recording of everything our parents say and do; we have no reason to disbelieve their values and actions – they are right. At the same time we record our responses; the child recording includes our instincts, biological urges, curiosity, intrinsic joys, sadness and desires. The parent is what we have to do; the child is what we want to do. However, the adult is our growing perception of the world through asking why and learning. It is thinking, predicting, problem solving and reasoning. The best communication is adult to adult, but when under STRESS we revert to parent or child. "Have you seen my car keys?" "Well if you put them where you could find them you wouldn't have to ask." "Oh, thanks a million!"

TA recognises five parental injunctions (drivers) which remain with us to shape our personalities: Be Strong, Be Perfect, Please Me, Hurry Up and Try Harder. TA was popularised by Amy and Thomas Harris, founders of the Institute for Transactional Analysis, in their book, *I'm OK, You're OK*.

TRANSFER OF UNDERTAKINGS

This is a complex area of LAW and practice. In essence, under the Transfer of Undertakings (Protection of Employment) Regulations 1981 (TUPE), which followed the EU Acquired Rights Directive 1977, if a business is taken over or merges with another business, the employees affected are entitled to be treated as stock in trade and move to the new employer with their contractual rights safeguarded. Any attempt to sack them or reduce their employment rights in anticipation of the transfer will usually result in successful claims for UNFAIR DISMISSAL.

Contracting out a function or service is usually covered by the same basic rules and any negotiation for SUBCONTRACTING will have to take these legal costs and issues into account. It is difficult to define a transfer and an undertaking; if in doubt, employers should seek specialist legal advice. It is, however, important to remember that the law's intention is to safeguard the job security rights of employees. There is little room for manoeuvre. If you acquire another company, you will have to accept the current employees' terms and conditions of work, probably for at least a year. The employees may, of course, voluntarily agree to a change within a shorter time scale, but even so the law checks that the agreement is genuine and the terms are not less advantageous than before.

The message is clear. Business transfers do not provide a quick or easy opportunity to change terms of work and saving on labour costs.

TRANSPARENCY

A word that is now widely used in employment matters. It means decision-making must be robust and backed up with evidence that it was done properly, that is in accordance with LAW and organisational codes of practice, and so on.

TUPE

Transfer of Undertakings (Protection of Employment) Regulations (see TRANSFER OF UNDERTAKINGS).

UNACCEPTABLE BEHAVIOUR

Using abusive or threatening words or behaviour, or distributing or displaying abusive or threatening material, can be a criminal offence if they are intended or are likely to cause violence, harassment, alarm, distress or stir up racial hatred. This is just one aspect of unacceptable behaviour that an employer must be aware of. It is important that the STAFF HANDBOOK makes clear that BAD LANGUAGE, BULLYING, FIGHTING, HARASSMENT, MISCONDUCT, RUDENESS, VICTIMISATION and VIOLENCE are unacceptable behaviour at work and will invoke DISCIPLINARY PROCEDURE.

People matter, and in the world of business, how you manage and relate to people is the key to success.
Dale Carnegie

UNDERTAKING

Another way of referring to an enterprise or business organisation. It can also apply to the public sector.

UNFAIR DISMISSAL

Most developed countries have laws protecting employees against being fired for an arbitrary reason. Protection against unfair dismissal was introduced as a statutory right in the UK in 1971 and now accounts for the largest number of claims to industrial tribunals. The popular perception is that each year thousands of employees take their former employers to the cleaners. The reality is different. It is hard to win cases and the amounts of COMPENSATION paid to successful claimants are normally low. The main hurdles former employees have to overcome to win are as follows.

1 They may have to show they have the required CONTINUITY of employment (currently two years). But a QUALIFYING PERIOD is not always required; for example, if a former employee alleges she was discriminated against on the grounds of sex, RACE,

DISABILITY, or being forced to work on Sundays.
2 They have to show that they were dismissed (see DISMISSAL).

If claimants can prove they were dismissed the employer has to establish a ground for the dismissal. If there are grounds the dismissal will probably be fair; if there are none it will be unfair. However, the employer has to show not only that there are grounds such as incompetence or gross MISCONDUCT, but also that, bearing in mind the overall performance of the employee in question, it was fair to dismiss (as opposed to disciplining in some other way). The grounds set out in the Employment Rights Act 1996 for a potentially fair dismissal are as follows.

1 CAPABILITY: including both the ability to do the job in terms of skills and physical capability. ILLNESS or disability, if major and long term, can provide grounds for a fair dismissal, providing the issue is handled properly (see below).
2 Conduct: such as LATENESS, VIOLENCE, dishonesty and other behaviour contrary to the employer's disciplinary rules.

There are some specialised grounds and also a catch-all ground of "some other substantial reason", such as lack of co-operation or generally disruptive behaviour. Employers must ensure they have and apply a proper DISCIPLINARY PROCEDURE before dismissing someone. Many employers with excellent and continuing grounds to fire someone nevertheless manage to snatch defeat out of the jaws of victory by failing to comply with these basic rules: employees should not usually be dismissed for a first offence; there should always be a thorough investigation; employees should have a chance to put their case (see *Discipline at Work*, an ACAS booklet). The LAW has established clear benchmarks for how most workplace problems should be handled before the decision to dismiss is taken.

Claimants who win their cases are entitled to

DAMAGES, which will have two elements: a basic award, a fixed sum directly related to their age, PAY and length of service; and an award for future loss, related to their likelihood of working again and other issues such as their PENSIONS. However, if an employee contributed to the dismissal in some way the INDUSTRIAL TRIBUNAL can reduce the sum. For most claims there is an upper ceiling of compensation of around £11,000. For claims where there was DISCRIMINATION or VICTIMISATION there is no upper ceiling; compensation of £150,000 or more is not unheard of.

The issues raised by the law relating to unfair dismissal indicate that:

- employees can claim even when correct notice periods are given;
- the reasons for dismissing or not renewing a contract have to be clearly established;
- appropriate procedures must not only be in place but also applied.
- there are some work situations, for example where discrimination may be alleged, that have to be handled especially carefully.

UNION DUES
A US term for a subscription paid by a member to a TRADE UNION (see CHECK OFF).

V

VERTICAL INTEGRATION
At its ultimate, the situation when a company directly controls everything in the process that affects it, from planning through acquiring components and assembling them to running the retail outlets where the finished product is sold. Despite its apparent attractions, companies today prefer a strategy that enables them to concentrate on their CORE BUSINESS which they support through PARTNERING or OUTSOURCING.

There are two different types of change; one that occurs within a given system which itself remains unchanged, and one whose occurrence changes the system itself.
Paul Watzlawick

VICTIMISATION
A form of DISCRIMINATION prohibited under both the Sex Discrimination Act (SDA) 1975 and the Race Relations Act (RRA) 1976 in the UK. Victimisation is defined as being treated less favourably than someone else in the same circumstances because it is suspected, or known, that the victim has brought proceedings under either the SDA or the RRA, has given evidence on behalf of someone else in similar proceedings, or has alleged that something has been done that contravenes either act.

VIOLENCE
For violence, or threats of violence against an individual in the workplace, see FIGHTING. Violence against property is covered by criminal damage under common or civil LAW.

VISION
"A picture of the success that will make the company's future" is just one of many definitions. Vision was a term first used by American management gurus during the early 1980s. Visions are normally created by the senior management team. Although the process of creating a vision state-

ment is important as it helps to clarify where the organisation wants to go in the future, if the concept is not shared by all the employees it will be meaningless. Sharing the vision ensures that employees have a clear view of the long-term aims of the business.

> *Idle dreamers have given true visionaries a bad name.*
> Robert Fritz

VISUAL DISPLAY UNIT
Commonly known as a VDU; but in all European legislation and HEALTH AND SAFETY literature it appears as DISPLAY SCREEN EQUIPMENT.

WAGES

Broadly, the money paid to employees by their employer for doing their jobs. Wages also include:

- statutory SICK PAY;
- maternity pay;
- HOLIDAY pay;
- any fee, BONUS or COMMISSION PAYMENT;
- payments ordered by an INDUSTRIAL TRIBUNAL which has upheld a claim for UNFAIR DISMISSAL and has ordered reinstatement or re-engagement;
- sums payable under an interim relief order made by an industrial tribunal in respect of continuation of a CONTRACT OF EMPLOYMENT;
- statutory payments in the form of:
- guarantee payments (payments made in accordance with the employee's contract of employment, or where there is no contract, the statutory guarantee payment provision);
- REMUNERATION for SUSPENSION FROM WORK on statutory medical grounds;
- payment for time off for antenatal care;
- remuneration under a protective award (the award applies where an organisation has failed to consult a TRADE UNION in respect of REDUNDANCY).

Excluded from the definition of wages are:

- advances;
- expenses;
- PENSIONS, allowances or gratuities;
- redundancy payments.

Wages may be paid weekly, monthly or at other intervals if appropriate, in cash, by cheque or directly to an employee's bank account. All such details should be in an employee's written STATEMENT OF TERMS OF WORK. In some countries MINIMUM WAGE agreements exist or are imposed by the government. Where this is not the case, an employer has control over the wages paid to its employees.

UK employers should note that around 17,000

people per year take claims to industrial tribunals relating to the non-payment of an element of wages.

Waiver clause

A clause in a CONTRACT OF EMPLOYMENT whereby an employee agrees not to exercise a statutory employment right in the case of REDUNDANCY or UNFAIR DISMISSAL. In most circumstances waiver clauses are illegal, but there are some situations where they can lawfully be used. For example, an employee on a fixed-term contract for one year or more can agree in writing to waive unfair dismissal rights; for two-year contracts redundancy rights can be waived. Similarly, an employee brought in to cover maternity leave can waive any rights when the employee whose work was being covered returns. Normally, however, employees cannot, even if they are willing, sign away their legal rights.

Warning

A way of bringing to an employee's attention that certain conduct or a certain level of performance is unacceptable. A warning is also something an employer must usually issue before dismissing someone to avoid losing an action for UNFAIR DISMISSAL.

Most organisations expect managers to give an informal oral warning for poor performance or MISCONDUCT. Where cases appear to call for immediate disciplinary action, or where an informal oral warning has already been given, the code of practice recommends the following.

- A formal oral warning should be given and recorded.
- If the misconduct or lack of performance is considered serious enough, or a formal oral warning has already been given, then a formal written warning should be issued and recorded. This warning should set out the nature of the misconduct and the likely consequences of further misconduct or

failure to improve performance.
- Further misconduct might warrant a final written warning, which should contain a statement that any recurrence of the misconduct or failure to improve performance could lead to suspension, DISMISSAL or some other specified penalty.
- When a warning is issued employees should be informed of any appeal procedures.

After a formal warning is given employees should be given the opportunity to improve their performance and/or modify their unacceptable behaviour. A review period and meeting should be jointly agreed, perhaps after four weeks in the case of poor performance. Details of the review meeting should be recorded in writing.

WEEK'S PAY

The starting point for calculating statutory COMPENSATION in the UK, where a statutory employment claim for, say, UNFAIR DISMISSAL or REDUNDANCY has succeeded. The formula is set out in the Employment Rights Act 1996. Where hours are standard the PAY will reflect this; where hours vary they will be averaged over the last 12 weeks of work.

WHISTLE BLOWER

A person who spills the beans about the organisation or individuals for whom he or she works, who has or is thought to have broken the LAW or behaved unethically. Whistle blowers are often sacked or suffer a DETRIMENT. There is no explicit UK legislation to protect them, although a bill is before the UK parliament. They do, however, have some legal protection under the Employment Rights Act 1996 if they blow the whistle on HEALTH AND SAFETY issues. Beyond this, it depends on whether they are seen to be acting in the public interest, in which case legal action or DISMISSAL would be considered unlawful. Defining the public interest is hard, but it does cover major frauds, corruption, sex scandals and conspiracies. The law is complex and still evolving. In the meantime, it would be unwise to penalise an employee who has a genuine concern about work. It is preferable to encourage open discussion, avoid cover-ups and aim to deal with the root cause.

WORK EXPERIENCE
See CAREERS SERVICES.

WORK OF EQUAL VALUE
See EQUAL PAY.

WORK PERMIT
EU nationals are free to work in any member state. Work permits are required in the UK for all other nationals. If in doubt, employers should check with the Department for Education and Employment and/or the European Commission.

WORK STUDY
See TIME AND MOTION STUDY.

WORKING TIME
The current trend is towards flexibility and open-ended working hours, especially for supervisory grades and above. Workers in the UK, the USA and Japan tend to work longer hours than those in other countries in the developed world. There is an established link between long unbroken hours and ILLNESS and accidents.

Until recently UK LAW has had few rules on working time. Employers have been free to require their employees to work flexi-hours or ANNUALISED HOURS, full time or part time, or any other variation. Employees had to accept work on the terms offered. A few occupations (drivers, pilots, and so on) had special limitations because of HEALTH AND SAFETY regulations. The EU Working Time Directive 1993 now applies to all member states. It requires adequate breaks from work on a daily (11 hours), weekly (35 consecutive hours) and annual basis (four weeks' paid HOLIDAY). In addition, employees should not, without agreement, work more than 48 hours a week.

Different rules apply to those working in the

emergency services and specific occupations, but working hours must still be arranged to ensure health and safety. Employers need to record working hours and prevent working hours causing STRESS. Failure to do so may lead to prosecution or claims for NEGLIGENCE if long working hours have caused illness.

> *The function of work is threefold. To give man a chance to utilise and develop his faculties; to enable him to overcome his ego-centredness by joining with other people in a common task; and to bring forth goods and services needed for a becoming existence.*
> Buddhist teaching

WORKS COUNCIL

A group of company and employee REPRESENTATIVES with established rights to information and CONSULTATION. In the UK employees have generally been represented by shop stewards belonging to a TRADE UNION, but in continental Europe representation has been mainly through works councils. During the 1990s trade unions and companies in the UK have become much more interested in works councils. This is partly a result of growing interest in stakeholding approaches to corporate governance; partly because of TRADE UNION interest in legally secured rights following the decline in members and influence in the 1980s; and more recently because of the obligation on larger companies with extensive operations in Europe to establish European works councils (EWCs) under the 1994 EU directive on information and consultation in EU-scale undertakings.

The directive aims to improve the right of employees to information and consultation through the establishment of an EWC or an alternative procedure. Organisations with at least 1,000 employees in the EU and at least 150 employees in two or more member states are required to establish an EWC. This is done on the basis of an agreement reached after the organisation has consulted its employees. Because of the UK's opt-out from the SOCIAL CHAPTER, UK companies based in the UK could exclude their British workforces from the calculation of these thresholds. Nevertheless, some 150 companies with UK headquarters were covered by the directive and most decided to involve their British workforces in consultation arrangements. The end of the UK opt-out will raise the number of UK companies required to set up an EWC to over 300, the largest single national grouping in the EU. EWCs are expected to embrace some 50,000 employee representatives throughout Europe once all 1,500 or so companies covered have established them. They could become the germ for European-level COLLECTIVE BARGAINING, although most companies and many trade unionists are either opposed or sceptical about such developments.

One of the most difficult issues is membership of the EWC. This is less of a problem where there is widespread trade union membership, but non-union staff should also be represented. EWCs normally meet annually. Reporting back to employees on the proceedings is an important part of the process, and in many organisations this involves using the existing systems of employee communication.

Research carried out by Incomes Data Services identified the key factors in the development of an effective EWC agreement as:

- establishing clear and open two-way communication;
- working in a co-operative spirit;
- being sensitive to different attitudes towards European integration;
- writing an agreement in terms that are easy to translate;
- setting up good translation facilities;
- keeping the agenda of the EWC to transnational issues;
- providing training for representatives;
- having an effective system of reporting back to staff.

In countries such as France, Germany and the Netherlands, works councils are not the main body for negotiating basic terms and conditions of employment (a right reserved for the trade unions). However, they do have extensive rights to information, consultation and sometimes participation in decision-making, and can sign workplace agreements on a range of subjects.

WRONGFUL DISMISSAL

Where employees are given no NOTICE of termination of their CONTRACT OF EMPLOYMENT or a shorter period than required in that contract they can go to a civil court (not an INDUSTRIAL TRIBUNAL) to claim DAMAGES. Employers can defend their action by proving that an employee's conduct (for example, THEFT, serious VIOLENCE at work) justified the action. Dismissed employees must be paid for any period of NOTICE to which they are entitled under their CONTRACT OF EMPLOYMENT, whether or not they are required to work during that period. If an employer fails to pay WAGES for all or part of the required notice period the ex-employee can sue for wrongful dismissal to recover the money owed (see also DISMISSAL)

Y

YOUNG WORKER
Someone under the age of 18 but who has ceased to be a child. In the UK the Local Careers Office has to be notified of young workers employed in factories. It is an offence to employ a young worker in a betting shop or in a bar. A 1993 EU directive on the Employment of Young Workers (those under 19), implemented in part as the Health and Safety (Young Workers) Regulations 1996, requires employers to pay special attention to HEALTH AND SAFETY issues for young workers, and makes it unlawful to require them to do NIGHT WORK or OVERTIME.

1 Abbreviations and acronyms

ACAS	Advisory, Conciliation and Arbitration Service
ARP	Appraisal-related pay
AVC	Additional voluntary (pension) contribution
BPR	Business process re-engineering
CAC	Central Arbitration Committee
CBI	Confederation of British Industry
CEDP	Committee for Employment of Disabled People
CEEP	Centre européen des entreprises publiques
CRE	Commission for Racial Equality
DAS	Disablement Advisory Service
DfEE	Department for Education and Employment
DRO	Disablement Resettlement Officer
DSE	Display screen equipment
DSS	Department of Social Security
EAP	Employee Assistance Programme
EAT	Employment Appeal Tribunal
ECJ	European Court of Justice
EOC	Equal Opportunities Commission
EP(C)A	Employment Protection (Consolidation) Act 1978
ERA	Employment Rights Act 1996
ERS	Employment Rehabilitation Service
ESOP	Employee share ownership plan
ETUC	European Trade Union Confederation
EWC	European works council
GMP	Guaranteed minimum pension
GOQ	General occupational qualifications
HSE	Health and Safety Executive
IIP	Investors in People
IPD	Institute of Personnel Development
IOM	Institute of Management
ITB	Industrial Training Board
ITO	Industrial Training Organisation
JD	Job description
JE	Job evaluation
LEC	Local Enterprise Council (Scotland)
LIFO	Last in, first out

MA	Modern Apprenticeship
MIT	Massachusetts Institute of Technology
MPP	Maternity Pay Period
NIC	National Insurance contribution
NLP	Neuro-linguistic programming
NVQ	National Vocational Qualification
OHP	Occupational Health Practitioner
OPRA	Occupational Pensions Regulatory Authority
PAYE	Pay As You Earn
PHI	Private health insurance
PIW	Period of incapacity for work
PRP	Profit-related pay
PTSD	Post-traumatic stress disorder
QWL	Quality of working life
RPI	Retail Price Index
RRA	Race Relations Act
RSI	Repetitive strain injury
SAYE	Save As You Earn option scheme
SDA	Sex Discrimination Act 1975
SERPS	State Earnings Related Pension Scheme
SMP	Statutory Maternity Pay
SSP	Statutory Sick Pay
TA	Transactional analysis
TEC	Training and Enterprise Council
TQM	Total quality management
TUC	Trades Union Congress
TULRA	Trade Union and Labour Relations Act 1992
TUPE	Transfer of Undertakings (Protection of Employment) Regulations
TURER	Trade Union Reform and Employment Rights Act 1993
TVEI	Technical and Vocational Education Initiative
UNICE	Union des confédérations de l'industrie et des employeurs d'Europe
VDU	Visual display unit
YTS	Youth Training Scheme

2 Professional bodies and associations

ACAS
Head Office (and Work Research Unit)
27 Wilton Street
London SW1 7AZ
Tel: +44 171 2103613
Fax: +44 171 2103645

Asociación Española de Directores de Personal
 (AEDIPE)
Moreto 10
Madrid
Spain
Tel: +341 4682217

Associação Portuguesa de Gestores e Técnicos
 de Recursos Humanos (APG)
Avenida do Brasil 194, 7th floor
1700 Lisbon
Portugal
Tel: +351 1 899766
Fax: +351 1 809340

British Association for Counselling
1 Regent Place
Rugby CV21 2PJ
Tel: +44 1788 578328

British Psychological Society
St Andrews House
48 Princes Road East
Leicester LE1 7DR
Tel: +44 116 2549568
Fax: +44 116 2470787

Commission of the European Communities
200 Rue de la Loi
B-1049 Brussels
Belgium
Tel: +32 22 991111
Fax: +32 22 950138/39/40

The Commission for Racial Equality
Elliot House
10-12 Allington Street
London SW1E 5EH
Tel: +44 171 8287022
Fax: +44 171 6307605

Zentralverband Schweizerischer Arbeitgeber
  Organisationen
Florastraße 44,
8034 Zurich
Switzerland
Tel: +41 1 383 0758

Confederación Española de Organizaciones
  Empresariales (CEOE)
Diego de León 50
28006 Madrid
Spain
Tel: +341 563 9641
Fax: +341 262 8023

Confederation of British Industry (CBI)
Centre Point
103 New Oxford Street
London WC1A 1DU
Tel: +44 171 3797400
Fax: +44 171 2401578

Confindustria (Confederazione Generale
  dell'Industria Italiana)
Viale dell'Astronomia 30,
00100 Rome
Italy
Tel: +39 6 59031

Conseil National du Patronat Français
31 rue Pierre 1er de Serbie,
75016 Paris
France
Tel: +33 1 40694444
Fax: +33 1 47234732

Deutsche Gesellschaft für Personalführung
   (DGFP)
Niederkasseler Lohweg 16,
4000 Düsseldorf 1
Germany
Tel: +49 211 59780
Fax: +49 211 5978505

Nederlands Vereniging van Personeelsbeleid
   (NVP)
Catharijnensingel 53,
Postbus 19124,
3501 DC Utrecht
Netherlands
Tel: +31 30 367137
Fax: +31 30 343991

The Equal Opportunities Commission
Overseas House
Quay Street
Manchester M3 3HN
Tel: +44 161 8339244
Fax: +44 161 8351657

Fédération des Entreprises de Belgique (FEB)
Rue Ravenstein 4
1000 Brussels
Belgium
Tel: +32 2 5150811

Greek Personnel Management Association
2 Karitsi Street
10561 Athens
Greece
Tel: +30 1 3225704

Health and Safety Executive
Information Centre
Broad Lane
Sheffield S3 7HQ
Tel: +44 541 545500
Fax: +44 114 2892333

Institute of Employment Rights
112 Greyhound Lane
London SW16 5RN
Tel: +44 171 7389511
Fax: +44 171 7389577

International Labour Office
CH 1211 Geneva 22
Switzerland
Tel: +41 22 7996111

IP
Hauser Plads 20
1127 Copenhagen
Denmark
Tel: +45 33 131570
Fax: +45 33 325156
Danish Institute of Personnel Management

Irish Institute of Personnel Management
35-39 Shelbourne Road
Ballsbridge
Dublin 4
Tel: +353 1 6686244

Ministero del Lavaro e della Previdenza Sociale
Via Flavia 6
00187 Rome
Italy
Tel: +39 6 4683

Occupational Pensions Advisory Service
11 Belgrave Road
London SW1V 1RB
Tel: +44 171 2338080
Fax: +44 171 2338016

Office for Official Publications of the European
   Communities
2 Rue Mercier
L-2985 Luxembourg
Tel: +35 24 99281
Fax: +35 24 88572

Royal Association for Disability & Rehabilitation
25 Mortimer Street
London W1N 8AB
Tel: +44 171 2503222
Fax: +44 171 2500212

Svenska Arbetsgivareföreningen (SAF)
Södra Blasieholmshamnen 4A
S-103 30 Stockholm
Sweden
Tel: +46 8 7626000
Fax: +46 8 7626290
Swedish Employers' Federation

Trades Union Congress
Congress House
Great Russell Street
London WC1B 3LS
Tel: +44 171 6364030
Fax: +44 171 6360632

3 Other sources of information

In addition to the organisations listed in Appendix 2, the following provide lists of publications. Members of the institutions receive monthly journals, and have access to extensive libraries and research facilities.

ACAS Reader
PO Box 16
Earl Shilton
Leicester LE9 8ZZ
Tel: +44 1455 852225
Fax: +44 1455 852219

The Stationery Office
PO Box 276
London SW8 5DT
Tel: +44 171 8730011
Fax: +44 171 8738247

Health and Safety Executive Books
Tel: +44 1787 881165

The Industrial Society
Robert Hyde House
48 Bryanston Square
London W1H 7LN
Tel: +44 171 2622401
Fax: +44 171 7061096

Institute of Employment Studies
Mantell Building
University of Sussex
Falmer, Brighton
East Sussex EN1 9RF
Tel: +44 1273 686751
Fax: +44 1273 690430

Institute of Management
Management House
Cottingham Road
Corby
Northants NN17 1TT
Tel: +44 1536 204222
Fax: +44 1536 201651

Institute of Personnel and Development
IPD House
Camp Road
London SW19 4UX
Tel: +44 181 9719000
Fax: +44 181 2633333

Institute of Supervisory Management
22 Bore Street
Lichfield
Staffs WS13 6LP
Tel: +44 1543 251346
Fax: +44 1543 415804

Labour Research Department (LRD)
78 Blackfriars Road
London SE1 8HF
Tel: +44 171 9283649
Fax: +44 171 9280621

The Tavistock Institute
30 Tabernacle Street
London EC2A 4DD
Tel: +44 171 4170407
Fax: +44 171 4170566

4 Publications

UK publishers that provide detailed weekly and monthly publications on employment law and human resources management practice are listed below.

Croner Publications
Croner House
London Road
Kingston upon Thames
Tel: +44 181 5473333
Fax: +44 181 472638

Gee Publishing
100 Avenue Road
London NW3 3PG
Tel: +44 171 3937400
Fax: +44 171 3937463

Incomes Data Services (IDS)
77 Bastwick Street
London EC1V 3TT
Tel: +44 171 2503434
Fax: +44 171 6080949

Industrial Relations Services (IRS)
Eclipse Group
18-20 Highbury Place
London N5 1QP
Tel: +44 171 3545858
Fax: +44 171 2268618

A useful publication is the *Personnel Manager's Yearbook*, which lists 9,000 UK companies and their personnel departments and gives details of some 2,000 recruitment agencies, 1,500 management consultants and 3,500 training organisations, as well as computer payroll and many other services. It is published by: AP Information Services, 296 Golders Green Road, London NW11 9PZ, Tel: +44 181 4554550, Fax: +44 181 4556381

Journals

In addition to the publications of such organisations as the Equal Opportunities Commission and the Race Relations Board, and the library services offered by the organisations listed in Appendix 3, the following journals and books may be helpful.

Benefits and Compensation International
Tel: +44 171 2220288
Fax: +44 171 7992163

European Management Journal
Tel: +44 1865 843000
Fax: +44 1865 843948

Harvard Business Review
Tel: +44 1858 435324
Fax: +44 1858 434958

Human Resources Magazine
Tel: +44 171 9161880
Fax: +44 171 9161881

International Journal of Human Resources Management
Tel: +44 171 5839855
Fax: +44 171 8422298

Management Skills & Development
Tel: +44 1895 622112
Fax: +44 1895 621582

Multinational Employer
Tel: +44 1252 726416

5 Recommended reading

Armstrong, Michael, *A Handbook of Personnel Management Practice*, 6th edition, Kogan Page, 1996

Armstrong, Michael, and Murlis, Helen, *Reward Management*, 3rd edition, Kogan Page, 1994

Barnard, Chester, *Organization and Management*, Harvard University Press, 1948

Belbin, Meredith, *Team Roles at Work*, Butterworth Heinemann, 1993

Bennis, Warren, and Townsend, Robert, *Reinventing Leadership*, Piatkus, 1995

Berne, Eric, *Games People Play*, Penguin, 1968

Binney, George, and Williams, Colin, *Leaning into the Future*, Nicholas Brealey, 1995

Bridges, William, *Jobshift*, Nicholas Brealey, 1995

Casey, David, *Managing Learning in Organisations*, Open University Press, 1993

Crainer, Stuart, *The Ultimate Business Library*, Capstone, 1997

de Bono, Edward, *The Use of Lateral Thinking*, Pelican, 1971

de Bono, Edward, *Parallel Thinking*, Penguin, 1995

Drucker, Peter F., *Managing for the Future*, Butterworth Heinemann, 1993

Firth, David, *How to make Work Fun*, Gower, 1995

Fletcher, Clive, and Williams, Richard, *Performance and Appraisal and Career Development*, Hutchinson, 1985

Foulkes, F.K., and Livernach, E.R., *Human Resources Management Reading*, Prentice Hall

Glass, Neil, *Management Masterclass: A Practical Guide to the New Realities of Business*, Nicholas Brealey, 1996

Gleick, James, *Chaos*, Cardinal, 1987

Hamel, Gary, and Prahalad, C.K., *Competing for the Future*, Harvard Business School, 1994

Hammer, Michael, and Champy, James, *Re-engineering the Corporation*, Nicholas Brealey, 1993

Handy, Charles, *Beyond Certainty: The Changing World of Organisations*, Harvard Business School Press, 1996

Harzing, Anne-Wil, and Rosseveldt, Jonis van, *International Human Resource Management*, Sage,

1995

Herzberg, F., Mausner, B., and Snyderman, B., *The Motivation to Work*, Wiley, 1959

Humble, John, *Management by Objectives*, McGraw-Hill, 1971

Johnson, Gary, *Monkey Business*, Gower, 1995

Jones, Pam, Palmer, Joy, Osterweil, Carole, and Whitehead, Diana, *Delivering Exceptional Performance*, Pitman, 1996

Jones, Stephanie, *Psychological Testing for Managers*, Piatkus, 1993

Juran, Joseph, *Juran on Planning for Quality*, Collier Macmillan, 1988

Kanter, Rosabeth M., *When Giants Learn to Dance*, Simon & Schuster, 1989

Kaplan, Robert, and Norton, David, *The Balanced Scorecard*, Harvard Business School, 1996

Kennedy, Carol, *Guide to the Management Gurus*, Business Books, 1991

Kenney, J., and Reid, M., *Training Interventions*, IPD, 1989

Kirkbride, Paul S., *Human Resource Management in Europe: Perspectives for the 1990s*, London, Routledge, 1994

Landsberg, Max, *The Tao of Coaching*, Harper Collins, 1996

Larson, Carl E., and La Fasto, Frank M., *Teamwork: What Must Go Right/What Can Go Wrong*, Sage, 1990

Leighton, P., *The Work Environment: The Law of Health, Safety and Welfare at Work*, Nicholas Brealey, 1997

Leighton, P., and O'Donnell, A. *The New Employment Contract: Managing Contracts Effectively*, Nicholas Brealey, 1995

Leighton, P., and Syret, M., *New Work Patterns: Putting Policy into Practice*, Pitman, 1989

Likert, Rensis, *The Human Organisation*, McGraw-Hill, 1967

Margerison, C.J., *Making Management Development Work*, McGraw-Hill

Maslow, Abraham, *Motivation and Personality*, Harper & Row, 1970

Mayo, A., *Managing Careers Strategies for*

Organisations, IPD, 1991

McGregor, Douglas, *The Human Side of Enterprise*, McGraw-Hill, 1960

Metcalf, H., and Urwick, L., eds, *Dynamic Administration: The Collected Papers of Mary Parker Follett*, Pitman, 1957

Mitchell Stewart, Aileen, *Empowering People*, Pitman, 1994

Neave, H.R., *The Deming Dimension*, SPC Press, 1990, through the British Deming Association, Salisbury

Ohmae, Kenichi, *The Mind of the Strategist*, Penguin, 1983

Pascale, Richard, *Managing on the Edge*, Viking, 1990

Phillips, Nicola, *Motivating for Change: How to Manage Employee Stress*, Pitman, 1995

Pollard, Harold, *Developments in Management Thought*, Heinemann, 1974

Revans, R.W., *Action Learning*, Blond & Briggs, 1979

Schein, Edgar, *Organizational Culture and Leadership*, Jossey-Bass, 1985

Schonberger, Richard, *World Class Manufacturing*, The Free Press, 1986

Sedgwick, Noble Lowndes, *The Guide to Employee Benefits and Labour Law in Europe – 1996/7*

Semler, Ricardo, *Maverick*, Century, 1993

Senge, Peter M., *The Fifth Discipline*, Century Business, 1990

Senge, Peter, Kleiner, Art, and Ross, Richard, *The Fifth Discipline Fieldbook*, Nicholas Brealey, 1994

Seymour, L., and Leighton, P., *No Smoke Without Ire: The Complete Guide to a Smoke-Free Workplace*, Management Books 2000, 1995

Taylor, F.W., *Scientific Management*, Harper & Row, 1947

Thorne, Paul, *The New General Manager*, McGraw-Hill, 1989

Torrington, Derek P., *International Human Resource Management: Think Globally, Act Locally*, London Prentice Hall, 1994

Tulgan, Bruce, *Managing Generation X*, Nicholas Brealey, 1996

Ward, Sue, *Managing the Pensions Revolution*, 1995

Weightman, J. *Competencies in Action*, IPD, 1994